Searching for Hope
in the Silence

Searching for Hope in the Silence

Jenna Stoker Wright

Copyright © 2025 by Jenna Stoker Wright.

All rights reserved.

No part of this publication may be reproduced, distributed, or transmitted in any form or by any means, including photocopying, recording, or other electronic or mechanical methods, without the prior written permission of the author, except as permitted by U.S. copyright law.

ISBN: 979-8-9928200-1-0

For privacy reasons, some names, locations, and dates in this book may have been changed.

Some Scripture quotations are from the King James Version (KJV) of the Bible, which is in the public domain.

Some Scripture quotations are taken from the New King James Version®. Copyright © 1982 by Thomas Nelson. Used by permission. All rights reserved.

Some Scripture quotations are taken from the Holy Bible, New International Version®, NIV®. Copyright ©1973, 1978, 1984, 2011 by Biblica, Inc.™ Used by permission. All rights reserved worldwide.

Book cover design by Tamara LaShure.

First edition.

Publisher's Cataloging-in-Publication
(Provided by Cassidy Cataloguing Services, Inc.).
Names: Wright, Jenna Stoker, author.
Title: Searching for hope in the silence / Jenna Stoker Wright.
Description: First edition. | [Martin, Tennessee] : [Jenna Stoker Wright], [2025] | Includes bibliographical references.
Identifiers: ISBN: 9798992820010 (paperback) | 9798992820027 (ebook)
Subjects: LCSH: Wright, Jenna Stoker. | Children--Death--Psychological aspects. | Loss (Psychology) | Bereavement--Psychological aspects. | Grief--Psychological aspects. | Mothers and daughters--Biography. | Families--Southern States--Biography. | Nurses--Southern States--Biography. | Hope--Religious aspects--Christianity. | Forgiveness --Religious aspects--Christianity. | Resilience (Personality trait) | Spiritual life. | LCGFT: Autobiographies. | BISAC: BIOGRAPHY & AUTOBIOGRAPHY / Memoirs.
Classification: LCC: BF575.G7 W75 2025 | DDC: 155.9/37092--dc23

Contents

Acknowledgments ix
Notes xi

Prologue 1

Part One
And For A Time, The Future... Became Silent!

1. Hope on I-40 7
2. An Unlikely Nursery 17
3. The Mundane in the Midst 25
4. Only Ten Percent 29
5. "The Patient Could Die!" 35
6. And Then... The Other Patients 39
7. Unprepared 45
8. A New Rush of Hope 49
9. Hopeless and Alone 53
10. Wrapped in Love 57

Part Two
And Then The Past... Became Silent!

11. Mom's Struggle 61
12. Mom's Transition 63
13. My Transition 67
14. Mama's Baby: Daddy's Maybe 71
15. An Opal 75
16. "Virginia" Moments 79
17. Cokes 85
18. Mom's Apology 89
19. My Apology 93
20. The Golden Circle 99

v

Part Three
And Then There Was... Hope!

21. Prayer for the Children	107
22. Prayer for the Child	115
Epilogue	123
Sources Cited	129
About the Author	131
From Tragedy to Treasure	133

To
Mandy and Mom
… Because I Remember …

To
Grace and Isobel
… So You Will Know …

To
All Who Grieve
… For There Is Hope …

Acknowledgments

I am forever indebted to and filled with love for the three men in my life: Earl Wright, my husband and life journey blessing; Earl Isaac (Zac) Wright, my son; and Wayne Douglas Stoker, my dad. They were and are sounds that helped break through the silence.

To my trial readers in different stages of the book, Lynn Alexander, Anna Clark, Patti Hendry Geci, and Carol Phillips, I owe a deep appreciation for your insight and care for this book and its people. To the creator of this book's cover, Tamara LaShure, I am forever grateful.

To my daughter, Lee Amanda Wright, and my mother, Virginia Paralee Wright Stoker,* I offer a heart of gratitude for the mother-daughter bond that is eternal.

I am blessed with, encouraged by, and thankful for the newest Wright generation of women: my young granddaughters, Grace Paralee Wright and Isobel Jelena Wright.

God is good! Read this book's epilogue! God is faithful!

*My mother was a Wright and married a Stoker. I was a Stoker and married a Wright. The two Wright families were not related.

Notes

The environment, protocol, procedures, and other observations at St. Jude Children's Research Hospital that are contained in this book are encapsulated in the year of 1977 and my memory from that time. Over forty years have passed, and certainly with these years of science and medical advancements, the St. Jude Hospital of 1977 is not that hospital of today.

Patients' names have been changed out of respect to them and their families. Other names may have been changed also.

Prologue

Recently, I read somewhere that the most influential institution in the American South is the family. I wasn't surprised by this sociological revelation, but it did cause me to further contemplate my own identity issues—a woman who came from a strong Southern matriarchal family with women who were often publicly overshadowed by the dominant family male personalities but who were unwavering in their quiet strength and power.

It has been several years now that I have felt an overwhelming void in my life—a void brought on by the deaths of both my only daughter and my mother. As my mother's only child, I lost the future and the past of my matriarchal line. And although I love the men in my life— a loving husband, a precious son, and a caring father—and the "new" women in my life—two cherished young granddaughters, I have an emptiness they cannot fill.

This fetus of emptiness was conceived in the somber dimming lights over my mom's casket at the funeral home. It birthed itself the weekend after my mom's funeral when in the midst of a lively male conversation among my husband, dad, son, and a male cousin—football, finances, hunting—I fell asleep, only to awaken when the family attention turned to my nodding head. As the only female in the room, I was hesitant to turn away from the male concern that I was sick and to inform the men I was just bored with their conversation.

Of course, I still had an aunt in the matriarchal line—six hundred miles away—and a female cousin I was close to—only two hundred miles away. I am sure for many women that combination could be enough. But I grew up in a time and place when both immediate and extended family often lived down the street or fewer than twenty miles away. It was a time in the American South when the family was close both geographically and emotionally in the wake of members' happiness and tragedy.

And my life has had its share of both. Maybe it is the tragedies that make us who we are. Someone once told me at the height of my grief after the death of my baby daughter, "Tragedies make you either bitter or better. It's your choice." I don't know; I think maybe tragedies make you bitter and then better—if you don't get too hung up in the process. It has taken over forty years for me to be at this point in writing about my daughter's death. Maybe I am approaching "better," or maybe I am just longing to remember her. I have not, however, been able to remember her life without her death. She died so young that to most people who knew us at that time or who know us now, her illness and death define her.

I can hardly remember her face—without looking back at a picture. And although some may find this statement unbelievable, my arms still ache, between the elbow and shoulder, when I envision her face—ache to hold her. The ache is not figurative or metaphorical. There is a real physical pain. When I open the box that contains her baby clothes, I smell her, the fresh, soft scent of an infant—after all of these years. It is a decorative cardboard box. I often wonder why her fragrance has not waned. I am not the only one who can smell the aroma of her existence; her father can too. But I don't hear her sounds, her cries.

Now, the sound that I can hear associated with her is the sound of the tires over the swollen road breakers on Interstate 40 between Jackson, Tennessee, and Memphis; winter's icy memory still permeates the long miles with flat farmland stretching in all directions. The silence of the traffic—few horns blow on rural sections of interstates—is overpowered by the consistent pound of the tires.

Part One

And For A Time, The Future . . . Became Silent!

Chapter 1

Hope on I-40

Sunday, December 11, 1977

The rhythmic thud of the space markers on Interstate 40 reverberated throughout the ambulance's patient compartment. The young attendant sat across the vibrating floor and did not take his eyes off the bundle I held in my arms. He stayed prepared to intervene on this trip at any moment of crisis. Unknowingly, however, I thought him rude to stare at our pain. The gossamer baby blanket, only weeks ago a baby shower gift from friends, covered our infant daughter, Mandy, fitfully sleeping. Not speaking a word, my husband, Earl, sat beside me. In the blackness of the night, this ambulance was racing us toward St. Jude Children's Research Hospital in Memphis.

BORN ON THANKSGIVING DAY, Mandy (Lee Amanda Wright) was the most beautiful baby I had ever seen. Most babies had red skin shriveled like a prune—but not Mandy. Her skin was white velvet from the moment she lay in my arms in the delivery room. The whiteness of her skin was accentuated by her jet-black hair, a gift from her daddy. We had expected a cute baby, maybe even a pretty little girl. But Mandy was beautiful—angelic.

The day after her birth, I was walking down the hall—meeting the exercise protocol for new mothers. Approaching the nursery window, I saw an older couple viewing the babies cradled in their glass bassinets. "What a beautiful baby." The man was squinting trying to read the name. "Wright, baby girl."

About the time I got to the window, Mandy's eyes opened, and although the nursery was sound proof, I could hear with my eyes her scream. A nurse rushed over and scooped into her arms my tiny baby in the pink blanket. The woman's practiced movements and her quick response gave me a sense of assurance. After all, Mandy appeared to be special to the nursery staff.

I had not been to the nursery that often. The baby was brought to my room several times a day for nursing, and the demands she made during those lengthy visits overwhelmed me.

Mandy screamed or sniveled most of the time she tried to nurse. After one such nursing session, a floor nurse offered me her diagnosis for my troubled baby. "Your daughter has a personality conflict with you. I've seen it before." She grimaced as she walked from my room.

I stared in disbelief as the heavy wooden door closed behind her.

"A personality conflict?" I sobbed to my husband that afternoon when he came to the hospital. "A personality conflict with my baby!" He put no stock in the nurse's comments and spent the next hour assuring me her diagnosis was errant, even ridiculous.

But, still, Mandy would writhe in her blanket, draw her limbs into her body, and then throw them out in an exploding burst of screams. I could not comfort her.

After three days at the hospital following the delivery, we were sent home with this baby who when she was not sleeping either looked at me with pained eyes or screamed until she became blood red. Nothing had changed from the hospital, but now my husband, the youngest son in a very large family, was with Mandy for extended periods of time.

"None of my nieces and nephews ever cried this much or this long," he said during the first night's stay at home. "I don't understand." Even though his comments worried me, I took some consolation in having someone else realize that Mandy had a problem. After all, I didn't think a newborn could have a personality conflict with both of her parents.

Taking strength from his assurance that the personality-conflict theory was ridiculous, I sought a more tangible explanation, and the doctor appointments began.

We started by taking Mandy to a local pediatrician.

She looked so healthy—eight and a half pounds at birth. Thus, I, the mother, must be the source of the problem. The local pediatrician zeroed in on the breast-feeding. Mandy should be on formula. Although I felt a sense of guilt and failure, I also felt a sense of relief—relief that this medical person had evaluated symptoms, diagnosed a physical problem, suggested a means to relieve the problem, and smiled while giving the prognosis. "She's a beautiful baby. Once she gets on this formula, she'll be fine."

The screaming did lessen, but there was never a time that Mandy seemed at peace with herself or with us. I charted the intake and out-put of her body on the formula. As a teacher, I relied on the power of writing—of recording the facts.

"She probably has colic. My (niece, nephew, grandchild, neighbor's baby—take your choice) had it. Drove the parents crazy." Friends and relatives were trying to help, so I read in my trusted baby book about colic and then dismissed that diagnosis.

But how could I tell them that Mandy seemed so far away when I held her in my arms and rocked her? I wasn't sure how she was supposed to feel in my arms, and I thought I would sound silly asking. However, I suspected she should not feel so taut and tense. Weren't babies supposed to be relaxed—primarily sleeping and eating? Mandy scared me. When she exploded in screams, her eyes blazed, and her body stiffened.

"She has red spots on her body," I reported to the pediatric nurse who answered my call a few days after the visit to the pediatrician.

"How long has she had them?" The nurse appeared to be writing on a chart.

"Well, they come and go. I noticed them yesterday. They came up for awhile and then disappeared." I hoped the nurse would tell me they were nothing to worry about, but she didn't.

"Bring her right on over to the office the next time they come out. Don't worry about an appointment."

I watched Mandy closely for the spots to come back; it was to be some time before they reappeared. When I rocked her and she was not crying, I searched her face, her eyes for some hint of solution. Her blue eyes pierced me and searched my face. What were they searching for? I was failing her, and I didn't know what to do to make things better.

The next day when she was screaming and flailing her arms and legs, I saw the spots again. "I'm on my way with Mandy," I told the receptionist, who I assumed was at some point expecting my call. But by the time I dressed and got to the door, the spots were gone. I called the pediatrician's office back and cancelled.

When the spots reappeared the next day, I was already dressed. I rushed to the pediatrician's office.

After a few minutes of examination, the doctor consoled me once again.

"She's a very light-complexioned child and is going to be sensitive to sunshine and even mood swings. When she gets upset, she will break out in a rash or turn red with anger or embarrassment. But she'll be fine."

So, I wrapped my week-old overly sensitive baby in her blanket, put a bottle of new formula in her mouth, and took her home. I thought it unusual for this pale child to be the offspring of two parents whose lineage was thought to include Native American ancestors.

Then late on her third Sunday afternoon in the world, I noted how warm her skin felt, and like any good parent, we took her temperature. Only a degree of fever but enough for me to call my mom, a nurse, who drove with my dad the seventeen miles to check on their only grandchild.

"Call the hospital and see if my doctor is there." Mom was rocking Mandy and trying to sound routine and calm.

"What do I say if I get him?" I asked while looking up the ER number.

Mom examined Mandy and didn't respond. So I dialed. I was put on hold at the ER desk.

Then I heard the doctor's voice, "Hey, Jenna, what's the problem?"

As I began to explain Mandy had a fever, Mom interrupted. "Tell him that the baby's hands are cyanotic, and we are on our way to the emergency room." She was wrapping a blanket around Mandy and those precious blue hands. Dad had already gone to the car, and Earl stood in front of me with the baby bag.

I rode with Mandy in my arms to the ER of our small, rural hospital—only three blocks from our home.

"What a beautiful baby." Mom's doctor's manner was reassuring. And the nurse cooed to Mandy and offered to take her from my arms.

I wanted to hand her to someone with confidence. Over the last two weeks, all of mine had eroded. I watched the nurse put her on the examining table. The doctor was gentle as he listened to her heart and examined her hands and feet.

"I'm glad you called. She's slightly cyanotic in her extremities. Probably nothing major, but I think we should check her out." The doctor wrote on the chart the nurse had handed him. "I'd like to call a friend of mine who is a pediatrician in Jackson and get him to observe her."

When he saw the panic on my face, he offered an encouraging prognosis. "Don't worry—she'll be fine. We just need to observe her and get this cleared up." He didn't identify the "this."

I picked up Mandy from the table and wrapped her in her blanket. The air in the ER cubicle was cold.

The doctor was away only a few minutes. "When I relayed to the pediatrician that Mandy was cyanotic and running a low grade of fever, he told me that it was not unusual for infants to react that way to fever."

I relaxed a little; maybe first-time parents *were* overreacting.

He continued, "But I told him, 'Hell, in all of my years in medicine, I haven't seen a baby reacting like this to fever.'"

The doctor must have realized how disconcerting his pronouncement was for parents, so he rushed on. "He said to bring the baby down."

I began to cry, but for once, Mandy was sleeping in my arms.

"I think she's going to be just fine," the doctor said again as he walked toward the door.

I felt exhausted as we drove back home to prepare for our overnight stay at the larger hospital in Jackson, fifty miles away. Maybe this pediatrician could help Mandy. Maybe we could get our lives to some form of normalcy like the other parents and newborns who too had returned to our neighborhood in the last few days. No screaming in terror from these serene babies.

When we got home, we packed a few things for Mandy and for us to spend the night at the hospital where yet another doctor could evaluate our daughter.

. . .

I IMMEDIATELY LIKED the Jackson pediatrician, a middle-aged, balding man with a big smile. His young nurse in her starched white uniform followed him with patient charts.

"What a beautiful child you have," she said as she looked over the doctor's shoulder at Mandy in a fitful sleep lying in the small hospital bed.

The doctor's cold stethoscope woke her, and she began to cry. He examined her and then asked us some routine-sounding questions. His confidence was contagious. He was in command of this room, and he was going to "fix" our baby. He zeroed in on the formula issue again.

He reached for the chart and wrote some orders for the nursing staff. Cordially, he shook my husband's hand. "I'm going to change her formula and observe her tonight. We'll run some routine tests, and you can go home tomorrow afternoon." He smiled, the nurse smiled, we smiled.

Within the hour, a lab tech came to take blood for the routine tests the doctor had mentioned. Then about twenty minutes later another lab tech entered the room.

"You look familiar," he said as he looked over at my husband on the couch. He and Earl discovered that they knew each other from my husband's work at the university.

"Why are you taking her blood again?" My first thoughts were that there had been a mistake—that he did not realize that someone else had already taken her blood and that he would apologize for the error and leave.

He ignored my question. When the needle went in, Mandy screamed but then settled down to quiet sobs. I gave her my finger, and she clutched it in her tiny hand that was free.

My voice rose, "Why are you taking her blood again?"

The lab tech looked over at my husband still sitting on the room's small couch and confided, "Her white count is high, and the doctor wants to get a retest on it."

"A high white count . . . that means infection, doesn't it?" I did remember a little from my zoology class.

"It could." He was now unwrapping the tubing and dropping the new vial into the carry box. "It sure could . . . or even something else."

Then the tech was out the door, and we made small talk while Mandy again slept.

Fifteen minutes later, we heard a tap on the door and saw it open. Two young women in white lab coats walked into the room and hurried to Mandy. One carried a tray brimming with lab supplies.

The larger of the two techs spoke, never looking at us on the couch. "We are here to take blood." When I walked over to the other side of the bed, I noticed that the smaller tech averted her eyes. She stared down at the tray and then at Mandy, who was now waking up with a vicious scream as the needle hit the targeted vein.

"Why are you taking her blood again? This is the third time for blood in the last hour."

"I'm sorry, sweet baby," the large tech cooed to Mandy, who was now in a wailing scream. The small tech kept her head bowed and said nothing for the remainder of the procedure. And then just like the young male tech, their measured gait to leave seemed to me to be more rushed than it should be.

I made my way over to pick up Mandy and cradle her in my arms. I was evaluating the information from the lab technicians—repeated blood work-ups, high white count, infection . . . or "something else." Mandy squirmed a bit and then relaxed again.

Soon the door opened once more, and Mandy's doctor and nurse walked into our room. The nurse had tears in her eyes. The doctor spoke, "Mrs. Wright, please put Mandy in the bed and come over here and take a seat on the couch with your husband."

I laid Mandy in the bed and started toward the couch. The pediatrician continued, "I am afraid I have some bad news . . ."

"She has leukemia?" I threw out the diagnosis I found to be the worst possible from the information I had and my knowledge of cancer.

He was taken aback by my words. "Yes, she does. Within the next few minutes, an ambulance will be here to take you to St. Jude's in Memphis. I've called. They're expecting you."

An unspeakable agony erupted from a part of me I never before knew existed.

AND THEN I was holding Mandy in the back of an ambulance on Interstate 40 as the sirens and lights carried us into the city of Memphis, caught in the decorations and celebration of Christmas. The green I-40 sign invited the ambulance onto Danny Thomas Boulevard and to St. Jude Children's Research Hospital. I had seen this exit before on pleasure trips to Memphis but had never expected to be taking it. The street quickly turned into the St. Jude's compound. The first recognizable structure I could see was a round gold-roofed building whose sign declared it was the home of ALSAC, the fund-raising branch of St. Jude's.

A circle drive brought us to the front door of the hospital. The attendant unlatched the ambulance doors. No one spoke. I pulled the blanket around Mandy as the December wind blew cold. When we reached the front portico, a St. Jude's nurse opened the doors and welcomed us into the warm lobby hall.

She made no effort to take Mandy from me. She put an arm around me and said, "Come in. This is a place of hope."

"A place of hope," her words reverberated in the hall. Hope . . . I felt as though I were already in hell. What hope could anyone here offer?

She led us to an elevator, which lifted us up to the sixth floor where an ICU room had been prepared. The nurse held out her arms. Earl hugged my shoulders and then stepped in front of me and shook his head yes. Mandy, exhausted from the earlier tests and travel, had not cried since we entered the hospital. Now she stretched, trembled, and screamed with incessant energy. The nurse scooped her quivering tiny body from me and hurried into the ICU glassed room where I could see another nurse take Mandy and unwrap her. I watched the two nurses undress her and slip on a generic white cotton hospital shirt. By now the glass doors were secure, and I was a spectator in my daughter's life.

LATER WHEN WE got to the parents' room on the sixth floor, I walked over to the long line of hospital windows whose view overlooked Interstate 40 with cars, trucks, vans, and fourteen-wheelers zooming by on their way to somewhere.

"What do you think the people in those vehicles are thinking about?" I asked Earl.

He joined me at the windows. "I don't know . . ."

"I wonder what their lives are like." I pressed my face against the cold glass and tried to see into the cars. They were going too fast and were too far away. "I hope they hug their children."

Chapter 2

An Unlikely Nursery
Early Monday, December 12, 1977

The nurse's voice called us away from the windows. She had more pressing issues than getting us into a room.

She opened the door. "This is a room for patients' parents. It's your room. I'll have the front office bring your bags."

I had forgotten about the overnight bag for the planned one-night stay in Jackson. I had given the first nurse Mandy's diaper bag. The ambulance attendant must have left our overnight bag at the front office.

I walked into the room—far from Mandy's inviting nursery at home on Cherry Drive.

There the furniture was white, feminine, delicate French provincial—a full bed, dresser, and chest of drawers. On top of the chest was a lamp with a man in a black top hat—like a circus ring master—holding red, yellow, green, orange, and blue balloons, which caught their color when the light came on. Stuffed animals surrounded and hugged the lamp. A porcelain little girl in a blue dress holding a white kitten was near the hanging white diaper storage bag. Inside the chest rested all of those baby clothes ready to cuddle and comfort our sweet girl.

The white baby bed offered soft sheets. A red-tipped quilted baby comforter featuring children playing and one beautiful little girl holding a handful of balloons hung on the side of the bed near a hand-knitted baby blanket. Next to the bed was a white wooden, slatted rocking chair with delicate gold leaves and four beautiful blue flowers etched into the wood. And completing the room was a framed crocheted print from Mandy's Aunt Carol with her advice:

"Cleaning and scrubbing can wait till tomorrow . . . for babies grow up we've learned to our sorrow . . . so quiet down cobwebs . . . dust go to sleep . . . I'm rocking my baby and babies don't keep."

THIS ROOM we now were in had a bed, a chair that could be slept in, a small table, and a phone that hung on the wall. The phone was not for local or long distance calls. For those, we would go to the pay phone at the end of the hall. This phone was for in-hospital communication to the adjacent room—the child's room that was linked by a thick glass window running the width of the room about four feet above the floor. There were curtains on both sides of the glass, so the child or the parents or the medical staff in either room could declare a time of privacy. The child's room had a prominent rocking chair where nurses could comfort their patient. The bed was close to the window making it easy to see into both rooms. There was a speaker system that could be turned on to allow conversations between the parents and their child. So, hearing and seeing were possible, but there was no means of touching.

This room arrangement reminded me of movie prison scenes where the prisoner and the visitor could not touch each other because of the glass that separated them. And for the first time since her birth, no longer could I hold my daughter at will.

I wondered how many parents before us had this room. How many children had pressed the button to hear familiar voices or see familiar smiles? Who would push the button for an infant? Who would be there to know when Mandy wanted to see her mommy and daddy?

"The rooms on this floor were built to protect our children here. After chemo, many are vulnerable to the most routine of diseases . . . A common cold can become serious," the nurse spoke as though she were apologizing.

I tried to tune out her voice. My mind was drifting back. Just a few hours ago, I was sitting in my home decorated for Christmas, rocking Mandy and worrying about getting our Christmas cards stamped and in the mail. I had already taken some to the post office and now tried to remember where I had left the other stack I was working on when Mandy's fever came up yesterday. Today . . . yesterday? Yesterday . . . it was early Monday morning now. Earl should be getting up to get ready to go to his office.

"We need to call your secretary," I said to him.

"There's a pay phone at the corner of the hall. The front desk on first floor can help you with any questions." The nurse was still paused at the door.

"Thank you." I heard Earl's automatic response and turned to see the nurse exiting the room.

I sat down on the bed and began to weep. Earl did not move from the door. My weeping moved to moaning and then a low wailing. Earl still did not turn from the door. The wailing softened into sobs again. And then he turned. His face was soaked with tears. He walked to the bed, sat down, and reached out to hold me. I fell into his arms where I sought comfort, but for the first time, I felt my body stiffen at his touch. I was angry. I didn't want comfort. I wanted my baby, and he was doing nothing to help.

I pulled away from him, stood up, and walked to the room's

interior window. "There is no reason to keep these open." I pulled the cord on the curtains to hide the empty bed.

Earl didn't speak.

When I turned from the window, I saw he was lying on the bed with his face buried in his folded arms. I moved to the chair and slumped into the stiff, hard leather.

I was overwhelmed with weariness.

Soon I heard his soft sleepy breathing. I looked at my watch and realized I had been sitting in the chair inert for at least twenty minutes. The weight of the last few hours pulled at my eyelids, and I was again drifting into a sleepy stupor when I heard a soft tap at the door.

"Come in," I said. I didn't move.

Earl turned over and then stood up to face a nurse from ICU. I recognized her as the nurse who had been waiting for Mandy in her room.

"I'm Savannah. I'm Mandy's nurse today. She's resting . . . If you would like, you can go in to see her now." The young woman smiled.

From the chair, I looked at her—smiling and confident, in control. Earl put his hand under my arm and tugged. I got up but pulled away from his yielding grip.

We walked down the hall and followed the nurse into an open area where we waited for the ICU staff to buzz us into the Unit. When the glass doors slid open, we stepped in, and I heard a crash of air as the door quickly closed.

Earlier when we had come to the Unit, I had not noticed the layout.

There were five windowed rooms opening into the main area where a nurse's station allowed medical staff to monitor the patients. I could see that three of the five rooms were in use—with Mandy in the one furthest from the door where we entered. A small room for the doctor on ICU duty completed the Unit. His shift included sleeping there at night.

"The air in Mandy's room flows outward; no airflow goes into the room as a means of germ precaution." The ICU respiratory therapist had joined us and spoke as she led us toward the room. I stopped as the doors automatically opened when we approached them. I crossed the threshold into that room, another level of hell for me.

I walked over to Mandy. She was so tiny in the infant hospital bed. Even this small bed was large for a newborn. Newborns with ALL, acute lymphocytic (lymphoblastic) leukemia, were extremely rare we had been told. I couldn't see her face clearly because of the oxygen box over her head. The box's hum informed me of her need for support in breathing. My attention was drawn to the IVs in her arms. I remembered just weeks before how much it hurt when the obstetric nurse had put the IVs in my arm before delivery. Although I had not heard Mandy's screams as the nurses secured the IVs in her arm, I saw their echoes as I peered through the oxygen box and into her face.

"Would you like to rock her? We've brought in a rocking chair for you." Savannah walked into the room and spoke with a measured kindness. I was struck by her compassionate voice but aloof manner. I wondered if the aloofness protected her from the emotional demands of a gravely ill child and grief-stricken parents.

She moved around Mandy as though she were dealing with a baby who had a slight cold and would be taken home shortly to her nursery. She encouraged me again. "Would you like to rock her? She can do without the oxygen for a few minutes."

"No . . . no, I am afraid I might hurt her. What if my rocking pulls out the needles . . . I'll just sing to her."

I put my little finger into Mandy's hand, and she squeezed it and kicked the blanket off her feet. I began to sing, "Jesus loves the little children . . . All the children of the world." She recognized my singing. I had sung to her since I knew I was pregnant. Her relaxing was obvious in the readouts on the machines beside her bed.

Earl put his hand on my shoulder, making a family chain.

I heard the glass doors open. I glanced back to see Savannah leaving the room.

I transitioned into a softer voice and sang a melody that had comforted me often when I found myself in the midst of questions I could not answer.

> *"Trials dark on every hand,*
> *And we cannot understand*
> *All the way that God would lead us to that blessed*
>   *promised land;*
> *But He'll guide us with His eye,*
> *And we'll follow till we die;*
> *We will understand it better by and by.*
> *By and by, when the morning comes,*
> *When all the saints of God are gathered home,*
> *We will tell the story*
> *How we've overcome;*
> *We will understand it better by and by."*
>
> From "When the Morning Comes" by
>   Charles A. Tindley

Earl did not sing. Singing was not a gift he considered was his. But his voice did not need to be heard for his silence embraced the words of the song and this moment in time.

But Mandy relaxed with my voice—oblivious to the despair in the words. I felt her fingers' grip loosening. She was falling asleep, hooked to and covered by a cornucopia of machinery. She almost didn't exist in the expanse of the sci-fi cubicle.

Earl whispered, "I think it's time to go now."

I had been oblivious to Savannah's re-entering the room. I couldn't believe I didn't hear the whooshing of the air as the doors opened, but there she stood behind us.

"She's beautiful." Savannah's voice was wistful. She moved to the machines and began checking the lines to Mandy.

"Has she been crying much?" I said.

"Not much. I come in when the monitors indicate she's crying. I'm going to take very good care of her, Mrs. Wright."

This woman was not my foe, but I resented her anyway. Not for anything she had done, but because she could do what I couldn't. She could be with Mandy at will.

"There's a schedule of times you can come to the Unit to see her. I'm sorry, but you can only see her for thirty minutes on each visit . . . Also only two people can come at a time."

I turned to walk out. There was a large round black-rimmed clock with a white face hanging on the left of the door. It was time to go.

"The doctor has ordered tests for later this morning, and he'll talk with you after he gets the results." Savannah directed her words toward the door, toward me.

Earl leaned down and kissed Mandy's arm.

"I love you, Mandy," I said from the door. We passed by the nurses' station and into the hall. Not a word was spoken until we closed the door back in our room.

Chapter 3

The Mundane in the Midst
Mid-morning, Monday, December 12, 1977

"Do you want to go and make the phone calls?" I said.

"Let's make a list of who needs to be called." Earl took a pen from his pocket and a notepad from the table beside the bed.

"My mom and dad . . . one of your sisters . . . your office and the church office." It felt good to be in control.

"After I make the calls, do you want to go down to the cafeteria and get something to eat?"

"Not hungry." I curled into a fetal position in the chair.

"We'll need our strength. Mandy needs us." Earl's voice drifted off into nowhere.

I dozed. The sleep was empty.

Twenty minutes or maybe an eternity later, I heard the door open. I uncoiled my legs to sit on the edge of the chair. Then turning toward the sound of rustling papers, I looked up to see a gray-haired woman with an administrative-assistant's gold badge on her shoulder. Clutching the crumpled list of names he had made to call, Earl stood beside her.

"This is Cindi from the office downstairs," he said. His face was red, and I knew he had been crying on the phone calls.

I didn't respond.

"She wants to talk with us about the services here and have us sign some papers." He looked back at Cindi, but his words were directed to me.

"There are several papers the two of you will need to sign allowing us to treat Mandy." Cindi flipped through forms. "Also, I have made an appointment for you to see the social worker here at the hospital." This woman was a take-charge person, but her voice was warm.

She handed Earl the papers. He sat down on the bed, so I moved over beside him.

"Please sit down." I motioned to the chair.

I looked at the papers in Earl's hand. We both read in silence. He signed them and handed them over to me.

I signed.

"I appreciate your concern, but why do we need to see a social worker?" I said. "Our insurance is in effect."

"Oh, that's no issue here. All of our services are free. No family is ever charged for their child's being here." Cindi seemed surprised by my comment.

I handed the signed papers back to her.

"The social worker is to help you deal with issues you will face, like your employer, your other children, your transportation, counseling . . . things like that."

"Mandy is our first child," I said.

AND THEN MY THOUGHTS WANDERED . . .

Our first child—the first grandchild of my parents, who had only me, and at the time the youngest grandchild of Earl's parents, who had seventeen children and a multitude of grandchildren! But . . . our first child would hold a unique place in each family—the "only" and the "youngest."

Earl and I had met at UT Martin as juniors and had our first date spring of 1969. Actually, he had made a date with three co-eds for the same Friday night and at the last minute broke the other two dates. I had always teased him about how close he came to missing me. We married two years later near the completion of our graduate study and the beginning of his university administrative career at UT Martin. Two weeks after we married, I had gotten a job teaching English at the local high school.

"What about your employer?" Cindi interrupted my thoughts. "Mandy probably will be in and out of the hospital several times while we're getting her into remission. Some employers are more supportive than others."

"I don't think that will be a problem," Earl spoke now. "I have several sick-leave days accumulated, and my boss is very understanding."

I could tell Cindi doubted him. She didn't respond but lowered her head.

"I'm on maternity leave for this year at the school where I teach, so there is no issue there," I said.

"Well, I've made the appointment for later in the week. You may think of some questions you have for our social services by then." Cindi stood, unabashed by our declarations of support, and shook hands with each of us. "Remember that you are in a place of hope. I will be thinking about Mandy. If there is anything I can do for you, just stop by the admissions office downstairs."

She stepped out of the door and gently closed it.

I moved back to the chair, and Earl lay across the bed.

She said "in and out of the hospital while they get her in remission." No one else had used that word . . . remission.

I closed my eyes. No sleep came. My mind was too full.

I knew that there would be several tests this morning and later Mandy's doctor would conference with us. But this woman, this Cindi, spoke to us as though Mandy wasn't about to die . . . but about to live.

I took courage.

"Let's go to the cafeteria," I said. "Is anyone coming down to Memphis to see us today?"

Earl stretched and then stood up. "Your parents are coming. They plan to go by the house before they come and get us some extra clothes."

"What about Dr. Dodson?"

"I called the church office. He's coming this afternoon."

We walked to the elevator. Earl pushed the down button.

"And I called my office. The secretary said Director Freeman and his wife are coming tomorrow or Wednesday."

The lights above the doors indicated that the elevator was five floors below us now.

"She said 'remission.'" I whispered as though I was afraid the word would disintegrate when spoken.

Earl took my hand and squeezed. "I heard. I think that's a good sign."

The elevator sounded its arrival.

I squeezed back. "Come on . . . let's go get some breakfast."

Chapter 4

Only Ten Percent

Early Afternoon, Monday, December 12, 1977

I heard a knock on the door.

"Come in," Earl was quick to respond.

The door opened to a young man clasping a medical chart to his chest and wearing a white doctor's coat. His stethoscope was folded into his right coat pocket.

"Mr. and Mrs. Wright?"

His hair was brown and thinning on top. His smile was gentle, and his voice quiet.

"I'm Dr. Gary Brodeur, Mandy's doctor." He thrust his hand toward Earl and then on to me.

"Dr. Brodeur, what can you tell us about Mandy?" I said.

"Mandy is a very sick child." He looked directly at Earl.

But I stared into his face, looking for more encouragement than his words had offered. I could observe nothing in his manner beyond what he was saying.

"Her white count is very high, and we have confirmed the Jackson hospital's diagnosis, acute lymphocytic leukemia." He looked to our faces for a recognition of the term. "The good news is that we have a reasonable percentage of success with this kind of leukemia. Many of our children here go into remission with ALL. And many make the five-year mark to be declared cured."

"Please sit down." Earl pointed to the chair I had left to move closer to him. We sat on the bed, and Dr. Brodeur sat in the chair.

"Then . . . that's good . . . that she has that kind of leukemia," I said.

"It is . . . Our problem is that Mandy is so young. We seldom see patients of her age with the disease this progressed." He crossed his legs and seemed to be preparing for a lengthy conversation. "The time-line of this disease indicates that she must have had the disease when she was born. But I want you to know that we will be doing everything we can to get her into remission." I noted that word again.

He continued, "We have made much progress with this disease. We'll give Mandy all the benefits of everything we know." He looked down at the chart and then up at us.

"Please . . . help her. We love her so much." I began to sob. "Her birth is an answered prayer . . . This can't be happening."

I could have said that her birth was an answer to a multitude of prayers. Like many couples, when we didn't get pregnant right away, we had worried that it would never happen. And thus, the petition to God to have a baby led our daily prayer list.

"I'm so sorry." He moved to the edge of the chair but no farther. "We will do our best. And I'll always try to be open with you about her condition and treatment."

Now he moved closer. He took my hand and covered it with both of his. "But you have to understand that Mandy's life is in the hands of someone much bigger than our staff here."

"Dr. Brodeur," Earl's voice quivered. "I know this is a place of hope—"

"It is," Dr. Brodeur interrupted Earl.

"But . . . what are her chances of getting well?"

"No one really knows that, Mr. Wright."

"I understand . . . she is in the hands of a higher power . . . you said that. But . . . you said a high percentage of success earlier. What are her chances of going into remission?"

The doctor lowered his head.

"Ten percent . . . she has a ten percent chance of surviving this."

Earl got up and walked to the window and looked into the adjoining empty child's room. "Only ten percent . . ."

"But, ten percent . . . There is hope. And as long as there is life, here at St. Jude's, there is hope." Dr. Brodeur squeezed my hand. "We will do everything we can for her. You pray, and we will work." He dropped my hand.

Earl walked back from the window.

"I appreciate your honesty . . . if not your prognosis." Earl had positioned himself directly in front of the doctor.

"I understand." Dr. Brodeur turned to the second page on the chart.

Earl moved to the bed and dropped beside me.

"Now, let's talk about the protocol we will follow in treating Mandy." Dr. Brodeur's voice attempted to sound positive.

I could feel the blood pulsating through my veins. My body throbbed with anxiety. My ears pounded with the sounds of the walls screaming in anguish. From the past words spoken to other parents here or the words being spoken to us . . . I couldn't tell.

I looked into the doctor's face to see if he heard the sounds in this room.

But he spoke with a calm, measured cadence.

"We will finish more tests today and then feed all of the results of the tests into a computer which will then determine what protocol should be followed for Mandy."

"I'm not sure I understand," my voice trembled. "*You* are not going to make the plan for her treatment."

He paused. All sounds were silent, except for the footsteps

outside, which halted at our door and then continued on down the hall.

"At this time, the procedure here is to rely heavily on the computer's information to make the decision. We have several protocols. One may be successful on one child and fail on another. And . . . we have not yet been able to determine why."

"Will you tell us which protocol she is on once the decision is made?" Earl said.

"Of course."

Dr. Brodeur stood up now. When he reached the door, he turned. "You pray. That's your part. And we'll do everything humanly possible."

"Yes," I could say no more. I saw Earl shake his head in agreement.

I heard the door close, and the doctor was gone.

"Did you hear someone outside the door when he was in here?" Earl said.

I moved back to the chair but didn't answer. I was already too deep in thought to hear another word. He had said that Mandy had leukemia when she was born. My mind was reeling. Did I have leukemia? Did I give Mandy leukemia? How could she have leukemia if I didn't have it? And . . . if she had leukemia, then I had to have exposed her to something that triggered it.

I began to think of our new home under construction. I had gotten sick at one of the factories where the contractor took me to look at marble for the bathrooms. I had almost fainted.

"I've given Mandy leukemia."

"What are you talking about?" Earl said.

"If she had it at birth, I ate something, took her somewhere, exposed her to something—"

"You can't think like that." Earl tried to hug me, but I pulled away.

"That's what the doctor said . . . 'before birth.' How can I think anything else?"

I was furious with the doctor . . . with Earl . . . with myself . . . with God.

And I couldn't be angry with God. According to Dr. Brodeur, a higher power was our only hope.

"Jenna . . . " I heard my mother's voice. She and Dad had been the footsteps that stopped and then continued after hearing voices in our room.

There was respite in my parents' being in the hospital, although they insisted on our going to the large visitors' area on the first floor to talk. To Mom she was helping—getting me off the sixth floor.

But the sixth floor went with me everywhere.

Chapter 5

"The Patient Could Die!"
Wednesday Night, December 14, 1977

It was Wednesday night and the last visit for us today in her ICU room. The chosen protocol was three-pronged and was dripping into Mandy's veins.

Earl and I stood beside her, now not recognizable as our child. The swelling was all over her body. Her face was distorted, and her enlarged fingers clung to my hand as I sang to her. Her beautiful black hair had been shaved in the front just above her eyes in an attempt to locate a vein that could support more needles for IVs. Now her oxygen box was covered with blue felt hearts that her day nurse had made and glued on. Her pained eyes gazed at me, and Earl completed the family chain with his hand on my shoulder.

"Trials dark on every hand . . . And we cannot understand."

I wanted to stay . . . I wanted to go. Peace eluded me.

Again, the white-faced clock near the door ticked away the time. Staying or going . . . there was no relief.

When we came out of her room, I saw the ICU doctor on duty.

"May I talk with you a minute?" I said.

"Sure. Let's step outside the Unit."

The three of us walked though the Unit's doors and into an open area leading into the hallway.

"Mandy is so much worse." I began to cry.

"You have to understand that we must give the protocol time to work." His voice was compassionate.

"But she's so swollen," I said.

"That's because of one of the medications in the protocol." His eyes looked for my response. "Her white count is falling, and we have to be encouraged by that. If we can get the white count under control, the chances of hemorrhaging will be greatly reduced. This will be a process—not an overnight change."

"I'm afraid she is dying." I could no longer calm myself and was weeping against Earl's shoulder.

"Mandy is very sick, but she is not dying. Let us work with the protocol. I don't want you to worry about her being at the point of death. She is not."

He sounded confident of what he was saying, and I began to slow my tears.

"I will tell you when it's time to worry. Promise me that you will trust me to let you know if we come to that point."

I nodded. Earl shook his hand, and we labored our steps back to our room. It was 9:30 p.m. by then.

About 1:00 a.m., I heard a knock on the door.

"Coming." I made my way over to the door and found an ICU nurse there holding a chart.

"Mrs. Wright, I need your signature on this form," the nurse said. "We need to have your permission to do a procedure that Mandy needs tonight."

"Is she worse?" My sleepy voice trembled.

"No . . . she's not any worse."

Earl had awakened. I sat down on the bed beside him, and the nurse continued to stand at the door.

I read through the standard lines duplicated on the form and then saw the words that had been typed in for Mandy's case. I could not believe what I saw: they were wanting to cut into her feet in order to place IV lines in her veins. Then my eyes fell on the final standard form lines, <u>Potential Result of Not Doing This Procedure</u>. And for the first time, I read the words: "The patient could die."

I remembered those precious soft pink feet that we had cuddled at her birth . . . but . . . "The patient could die."

There were many levels of hell. I signed and dated the form.

The nurse went back to ICU, but we didn't sleep.

Chapter 6

And Then ... The Other Patients
Friday Morning, December 16, 1977

Darcy died today—Friday, December 16. She was in the ICU room across from Mandy. Only yesterday her grandmother told my mom that Darcy wouldn't die, that she couldn't. Darcy was too good to die. As a teenager at St. Jude's, she had been an ever-present inspiration to both patients and staff.

Mom struggled to avoid a confrontation on the subject of goodness overpowering death. After all, if that were the case, she concluded our tiny infant would prevail. But by sharing her response to Darcy's plight, I knew Mom, the proverbial nurse, was letting me know not to engage in such futile logic with Mandy's life on the line.

And so Darcy died. The ICU doors that locked in the air could not lock her in or death out. The thick glass, the pressurized air returns, the automatic doors, the watchful nurses, or the trained doctor on duty could not protect her from death when it chose to enter the Unit. It moved freely among all of the barriers. All was hopeless. And Darcy was gone.

It was a Friday that Darcy died, the end of an endless week. I followed my daily routine of breakfast in the cafeteria where the staff in the serving line would ask about the baby's night—no specific medical questions. There was an unspoken boundary for their inquiries. At the small table, I usually took a few bites and then moved my food around in widening circles on the plate. But seeing the bright lights of the cafeteria this morning and people who appeared refreshed by the night's rest assured me of a new day.

Christmas ornaments, trees, and wreaths decorated the lobby and cafeteria. Moving among the bright decorations were the children. Some there for chemo—heads bald, eyelashes and eyebrows nonexistent. Some faces were marked by pain and fear. Others by quiet smiles. Some laughing children returned from check-ups—declarations of remission or cure—a real Christmas present. But all parents' faces were marked by anxiety. Still, the hospital was electric with the energy of a city and its people caught in the celebration of Christmas, of hope. These were the children of hope. These parents understood the significance and the limits of hope.

I got some coffee and took the tray with whatever breakfast food the kind serving-line workers had put on my plate. Earl and I found a table near a family whose small son appeared to be at the hospital for a check-up. He was drinking orange juice, ignoring his breakfast food, and playing with a truck while his parents emptied their cups of coffee and ate their breakfast rolls.

I wondered if Mandy too would come back someday for check-ups—our family staying at a local hotel and coming in for tests to make sure she was still in remission. Mom told me yesterday she was envisioning Danny Thomas with Mandy as the poster child for St. Jude's. I had let myself hope, just a little, when she told me her thoughts.

But now I remembered last night and our friend Charley.

. . .

His twelve-year-old daughter Kaley was on a return visit to St. Jude's—battling her liver cancer. We had met him on our first day at the hospital and found him to be an encourager. "Sure, the odds might be against us, but miracles happen here at St. Jude's," he assured us.

I liked Charley. When he smiled, there was hope somewhere out there. Both he and his wife were teachers in Florida, and she was at home with their younger son while Charley and Kaley were here in Memphis where the doctors were trying to get her back into remission.

When Charley, who had flown into Memphis and thus was at St. Jude's without a car, asked if Dad could take him to a Colonel Sanders' to get Kaley some Kentucky Fried Chicken at ten last night, my dad said yes. He hurried to get his car and rushed to the closest restaurant before it closed. It was the first food Kaley had asked for since her arrival several days ago.

When Dad and Charley got back with the chicken and all of its trimmings, Charley gave the nurse the plate to take to Kaley and rushed into his parent's room to watch her eat.

Earl and I made our way down to the small waiting room on our floor to break the monotony of our cubicle and to be able to sit with Mom and Dad, who had just returned from his mission of mercy with Charley.

While there talking, we heard the first sounds of crescendoing moans. Earl walked out into the hall, and I saw him turn and then disappear. The moans were now loud sobs, and as I entered the hall, I saw Earl going into the men's bathroom, the evident source of the sounds. Mom, Dad, and I stood in the hall and stared at the bathroom door until Earl emerged with Charley wiping his eyes with his white handkerchief.

Charley looked at me, the mother he had indicated just might receive a miracle.

"She wouldn't eat any . . . not even one little bite." And he broke into shaking sobs again.

I hugged him. I was realizing that here at St. Jude's, the parents as well as the patients needed a miracle.

He stood with us a few minutes and then made his way back into his half of Kaley's room. I watched him pause in front of the door, wipe his eyes, put his handkerchief away, and smile. It was a forced smile—not believable to us there in the hallway with him, but I guessed the thick glass and Kaley's condition would make it believable to a young girl whose body was wracked by cancer.

My thoughts changed as the little boy's truck crashed to the floor, and I jumped at the sound. His dad picked up the truck and then his son and made their way into the hall. I took another drink of my coffee. Today, I didn't even pretend to move the food around on my plate. Just let it lie there. It was Friday.

Earl finished eating and then took my tray with his. It was time to go back up to our cubicle and wait until visitors were again allowed into the ICU.

When the elevator reached our floor, we passed Mrs. Parks, Vernon's grandmother. She lived in the room on the right of ours. Unlike us, she had a child on the other side of the thick glass—her grandson Vernon. Vernon was not yet of school age. I guessed him to be four. We had stood at the door and talked with Mrs. Parks earlier in the week and had seen Vernon in his bed on the other side of the glass.

"I can hardly stand it when he cries for me to come over and rock him," the elderly Black grandmother had confided to us—with the sound turned off to Vernon's room.

We didn't respond. What could we say as tears began to make a path down her wrinkled face, we who just hoped to have the opportunity to see Mandy one day out of ICU and not through a glassed wall.

But today, Mrs. Parks looked even more strained as she nodded her head and boarded the elevator. We spoke and moved back to the inertia our sixth floor room held. Sometimes I felt relieved to have that inertia. After all, there was a strong possibility that things would get worse rather than better.

"Someone is crying," Earl said just as we got to our room.

I stopped. "It's coming from next door."

He turned toward Vernon's room and listened.

"It's Vernon. Mrs. Parks must've left the speaker on when she went down for breakfast." Earl was already walking over to the door, which was ajar.

He walked into the room, but I paused in the doorway.

"Hi, Vernon. Are you OK?" Earl's voice was kind and invited conversation with the four-year-old.

"Where's Mi-Mi?" Vernon sobbed. "I want Mi-Mi."

"She's gone to breakfast. She'll be back in a few minutes."

"I want her to come hold me."

His bed was close enough to the glass that I could see the ravages of pain on his face. "My stomach hurts."

"Do you want me to call the nurse?" Earl knew from Mrs. Parks that Vernon was on heavy pain medication, and he remembered where the buttons were for contacting the nurse who was on Vernon's side of the glass—although the buttons in our room remained untouched.

"I want Mi-Mi to hold me."

"How about if I sit here and tell you a story until Mi-Mi returns?"

Vernon's sniffles began to subside. "What kind of story?"

As Earl moved to the chair, I backed out of the doorway and started for our room.

When Mrs. Parks returned minutes later, she again assumed her vigil, and Earl joined me to face another day with Mandy.

Our friends and family had been coming all week—not staying long at any one time. The sadness was too overwhelming to endure for long. Only Carol, a friend, listened to my pain for an entire day—bless her ears and heart. Others went back home and organized prayer vigils, and others gave blood in Mandy's name. They came; they left to go home to do what they could to help. We stayed; there was nothing we could do but hold her hands and sing to her.

The day passed with few events—other than a bone marrow exam. Someone once told me that babies suffer less because their cells for pain are not fully developed at first. Probably a myth. Some grown-ups say the pain is excruciating in a bone-marrow exam. Mandy couldn't tell us. Anyway. . . I am not sure I could stand to know.

Chapter 7

Unprepared

Friday Night, December 16, 1977

Then it was night again, Friday night. The nights were the worst. Nine o'clock was the last time we could visit Mandy in ICU. All of our family and friends had gone home to refresh for whatever the weekend had in store. Earl and I were alone. We were always alone. Even when surrounded by friends and family, I was very alone. No one, not even Earl, could reach the depths of my sorrow. Nor could I reach his.

We approached the secured doors of the ICU, and Earl pressed the button to let the staff know we were there to see Mandy. The doors didn't open. He pressed again. Nothing.

I tried to see into the Unit but couldn't. Neither could I see medical staff moving around as I sometimes could when we waited.

Earl pushed the button again.

"Something's wrong." I began to cry.

"It may not be Mandy." Earl hugged me.

I heard the doors opening as I buried my face into his shoulder. When I turned, I saw the ICU doctor.

"Mandy is not doing well," he said.

I heard the labored sound of a machine coming down the hall and turned from the doctor to see a small respirator being pushed toward the Unit.

"Is that for Mandy?" I couldn't take my eyes from the medical team in a run pushing the machine.

"Yes," the doctor said as he pushed a code to open the ICU doors for what would be my daughter's last hope. He was the doctor on duty—not Mandy's doctor, who was off for the weekend. But we had talked with this doctor several times before now.

He turned to face us. Before he could say anything, Earl spoke.

"You told us not to worry until you told us to. Should we worry now?"

"Yes, Mr. Wright, I'm afraid so."

Hearing my scream, one of the nurses from the Unit rushed out to us, and the doctor was back in the Unit before we could ask more.

The nurse directed us to a small room near the ICU. I had never noticed the room before. I guessed the doors were usually closed. It was kept for just such times as this.

Earl was weeping. He guided me to a chair and sitting down pulled me over to him. Weeping together we waited.

Moments later with the nurse at our side, the doctor returned to us. "She is hemorrhaging; we are struggling to stop the bleeding."

"Is she dying?" I asked.

"Yes." This time he did not lower his head, but his eyes engaged mine as he searched for what he could say to offer hope. Hope, a balm in life and in death.

I began a litany of sobs that can emerge only from the heart of a parent losing a child at that moment. At first, I was uncontrollable.

"Please, Mrs. Wright, remember that we talked of this possibility. You put her life in God's hands. You said you were prepared if she could not live." The doctor's voice was pleading. The nurse was crying.

I knew I had said exactly what the doctor was repeating. And I meant it at the time I said it to him. After all, I had been raised in the Christian faith. I accepted that God was sovereign, so she could rest in only His hands. I accepted that she was covered by the grace of Jesus as an infant, so she would go to Heaven. Yes, I accepted that she was prepared, but what I had not realized earlier... I was not prepared... not prepared to let her go.

I muttered, "I was mistaken. There is no preparation for this." I hid my face in my hands.

The doctor's head lowered again.

Like a runner making her last effort to get to the finish line, frenzied I spoke, "Promise me that you will try to the very end. Do not unplug her. *Everything* must be done to save her."

"I promise you we will work with her until . . . there is no possible reason to work." With that commitment, he left the room.

Chapter 8

A New Rush of Hope
Friday Night, December 16, 1977

We sat in silence with the nurse for several minutes, and then I heard myself saying in a voice I did not recognize, "We need to make some phone calls."

Somebody out there had to know she was dying. The living had to be told. I felt as though I were being pulled apart. There was the dying to be dealt with and the living to be dealt with. I was being left with the living, but I wanted to go with the dying.

We made three phone calls. My parents and Earl's sister got the first two. They could get out the news. The third call was to a Memphis church layman whom we didn't know but who had left his card on our cubicle door as an outreach. Our pastor and church friends were two hours away, and we needed spiritual support.

When the layman arrived, he offered little with his everyday conversation topics.

He seemed to think if he didn't mention our child was dying across the hall, she just might not die. He was not prepared for our situation. At one point, he inquired of medical personnel in the room about the progress of another St. Jude's patient that he knew from his community.

I quickly realized this man had no training to deal with a dying child's parents although his intentions were noble. Later, I would advise pastor friends that churches must prepare lay people for spiritual counsel that they entrust to them.

But now, I actually felt sorry for him.

"It's getting late. We may be in for a long night. Go on home to your family," I murmured.

"No, I don't mind staying. I'd just be watching Johnny Carson if I were home." His strong voice carried across the room as he settled into his chair with a sense of obligation and nothing-better-to-do attitude.

I placed my hand on Earl's hand and patted. I had seen the anger on his face—his daughter was dying, his wife was inconsolable, and this man had no clue to what he was witnessing.

Realizing the layman's good intentions but his ineptitude, the nurse with us asked if she could call Father Brian from a church close to the hospital where he routinely ministered to parents and patients at St. Jude's. We agreed for her to make the call.

When he arrived, Father Brian was prepared for us. He held our hands, speaking little, and mourned with us.

The only consistent conversation came from the layman—talk about nothing that mattered to us. His words hung in the air waiting for response which never came.

Soon the doctor came in again. He was somber.

"I'm sorry. We did all we could. We couldn't stop the hemorrhaging from her lungs . . . She's gone."

Earl and I wept.

"May we see her?" I wanted to touch her one more time.

"As soon as they get her cleaned up, we'll take you in." The doctor started to leave but paused at the door.

"I know there is never a good time to say this to parents, but we would like to ask your permission to do an autopsy on Mandy. So few children her age have leukemia this advanced, and we would like to study her to see if our research on her can help other children."

"I don't know." I couldn't believe I was considering saying no. Mandy was gone; nothing else could be done for her or to her. Yet, it hurt me to think of her body undergoing an autopsy.

"Jenna . . . she's gone." Earl was wiping the tears that covered his face. "If someone else can be helped, let her make that gift."

I turned to Father Brian; he had been here with parents before. My mind was racing. I just couldn't phantom the procedure on my precious baby. He shook his head "yes."

The doctor took my hand. "It'll be done like surgery. I can assure you that her body will be given the respect you want."

I dropped my head in agreement.

The doctor slipped from the room.

Father Brian looked into my grieving eyes and said, "The angels must have broken through the roof of St. Jude's with Mandy in their arms."

And I experienced a new rush of hope!

Chapter 9

Hopeless and Alone
Friday Night, December 16, 1977

Her final battle with the ravages of cancer had lasted only two hours. Neither the staff nor we had been called on to make long-range decisions about life-support. We were spared that task. So, we waited, no one speaking. The only sounds to be heard were quiet cries from Earl and me, and an occasional sigh from the layman. He had not left although encouraged to go. He stayed in the room between his sense of obligation and the mesmerizing trance of observing those caught in tragedy.

Soon the door opened again, and the doctor walked over to Earl and me. "You may go in now."

Father Brian supported me on one side, and Earl supported me on the other. The layman, the nurse, and the doctor followed one at a time behind us—like travelers on a pilgrimage. This time the doors opened as soon as we approached. We were expected.

Two of the ICU nurses came and hugged me as we entered the Unit.

The doors to her room were totally open now . . . nothing left to protect her from.

She was lying in the small hospital bed and was wrapped in a soft pink baby blanket. Her black hair had been washed and brushed. Her soft bangs were gaped where they had shaved her head in an attempt to run IVs.

I thought my heart would burst. With shaking hands I reached out and took her small hand that had clutched its tiny fingers around my little finger. Earl put his hand on top of mine—the three of us together one last time.

"She is so cold," I said.

No one responded. A few minutes later, the small group walked back out of ICU and down to the room where Earl and I had spent the last few days.

She was gone—never would I see her on the other side of the thick-glassed window in our room. I would never hear her coo or cry over the speaker. Never would I sing her songs again. Never would I hear her.

Mandy was silent.

And now there was only the living to deal with—my parents and Earl's boss and his wife were en route to Memphis when Mandy died. The hospital's front office stopped them at the door to tell them she was already gone.

Earl and I were in the sixth-floor waiting room with all of our bags packed, including Mandy's baby bag, when they arrived.

I heard them get off the elevator. A hospital staffer walked them to us. Tears flowed in abundance. Father Brian and the nurse were still with us—only turning us over to family who must now bear with us the grief that would never end. Charley came to hug us before we left. Mrs. Parks wasn't told; she was asleep and too exhausted to be awakened—other than by Vernon's pleas. Darcy's mom and grandmother had left during the afternoon to accompany her body back to the East Coast.

We rode down to the first floor. Mom and I were alone for a

few minutes while others were in bathrooms and at snack machines.

"Your dad said we are going to be buried wherever you bury Mandy."

"Bury... Eastside in Martin..."

Bury... we were going to bury my baby.

"I'm glad. I can be buried at home." Mom avoided looking at me.

Martin was always her home although she had not lived there in over thirty years.

And in the midst of all of this tragedy, she was calmed that she and Mandy would rest together at home in Eastside Cemetery in Martin.

I didn't begrudge her any comfort she could find as we readied to leave St. Jude's—to leave without Mandy.

We paused near the cafeteria where in the morning the news would sweep through the serving line that "the baby" had died. I tried to take it all in—the sights, the smells, the sounds of the lobby at 2 a.m. As we walked through the foyer where the nurse only days ago had admonished us, "This is a place of hope," I felt hopeless and alone.

Chapter 10

Wrapped in Love

Sunday, December 18 ... Christmas 1977

Mandy was buried on Sunday, December 18. I remember little of the next few days except one afternoon when I threw all of the bouquets of carnations and other sweet fragrance flowers out the back door of the utility room. The house nauseated me with the aroma of the funeral home.

On the Friday before Christmas Eve, Earl and I had dinner with Mom and Dad. Sitting at the table picking at my food, I paid little attention to the conversation—so mundane.

"Jenna, did you hear me?"

Mom interrupted my thought inertia. I looked up at the three faces staring at me.

"What?"

"I asked what would you like for Christmas?" Mom smiled and reached to pat my hand lying by my plate. Her voice lifted, "We will get you anything you want."

"I want my baby. Can you get me that?" I spat the words onto the table.

Mom's face, furrowed from her own sleepless nights, fell in hurt. And I didn't care.

There was no baby to wear the soft red Santa hat we had purchased for Christmas morning, the Christmas cards signed "Earl, Jenna, and Mandy" would soon find their way into the Christmas trash at the homes of family and friends, and the Baby's First Christmas ornament had no baby to treasure it in the coming years. No baby . . . no Mandy . . . only silence.

"I'm sorry. No, I can't give you Mandy . . . Oh, that I could." Mom left the table and the room.

Earl and Dad sat with me in silence and gave semblance of continuing with their meal.

I don't remember Christmas Eve. I do remember Mom gave me a beautiful pair of dress boots—said she had already bought them back in November. That is the only Christmas gift I received that year. I don't think I ever thanked her for them although I did wear them often during the cold, snowy January and February that followed—a record-breaking year for snow and ice in West Tennessee. To this day, I hate to wake to snow covering the yards, roads, fields—no traffic, no movement, only a blanket of white, deafening silence.

Cold followed by silence.

But with the boots, Mom alone wrapped me in a tangible love. There was just something about those boots that made me wear them until the warmth of spring demanded sandals and tried to resurrect my heart with the promise of new life.

That was Mom—always wrapping me in love.

Part Two

And Then The Past . . . Became Silent!

Chapter 11

Mom's Struggle

I had been away from my hometown for many years before I would understand how very conflicted my mom had felt in the small Southern town where I grew up. She was conflicted by her respect, compassion, and love for the people there—many who had been her hospital patients before she married my dad, settled into his hometown, had me, and left her profession to raise me—and her desire to have a different life for me. From supervising nurse at the largest hospital in the area, she settled into housewife and mother in the early years of my parents' marriage. And on two different occasions when I was a child, she worked short-term in local factories as the designated factory nurse, but in each job she also worked on the line or in a supervisory capacity. There was not enough demand for a full-time factory nurse. There, she observed how many of the women in the factories were the primary breadwinners although they were not so recognized. She asserted her "stand" once when Dad considered doing more farming as a means of making a living. I can even now hear her listing the names of the women at the clothing factory whose husbands believed they made a living on the farm.

By the time I was in late elementary school, Dad was the broker in one of the two real estate businesses in the whole county. He bought and sold farmland—even rented some out to local farmers—but did very little row cropping on his own. Mom saw to that. She ran his office out of our home—receptionist, bookkeeper, scheduler, accountant. Dad was the salesman. She often told me, "Wayne could sell ice to someone living at the North Pole, and I couldn't give 'em a heater."

Maybe not.

Dad had good looks, a quick smile, a charming personality—if he liked you—and an ability to psychologically evaluate your "buying" personality. She was right—he could sell you just about anything. One of his real estate lines that always got a laugh sometimes haunts my memory. "I'll sell anything except my wife and child—and sometimes I might consider my wife." The customers always laughed at that one.

I don't think Dad ever thought anything about his real estate business joke. It endeared him to the men who were looking at property, and at that time, most of the women laughed too. But sometimes I thought I saw the hurt in my mom's eyes, and I never remember hearing her make any comment when that line was used in her presence.

Perhaps because of her reticence to respond in a family setting to her often being at the heart of Dad's real estate joking banter, I didn't always have the respect I should have had for her role as a Southern woman during a time when that perception was about to undergo major change. Neither did I grasp the significance of those ideals that she was pouring into me that would enable future generations to break out of the mold that Mom was struggling against.

Chapter 12

Mom's Transition

My earliest childhood memory of Mom is of her sitting in a plaid platform rocker in a corner of our first home, a two-story red brick on a sloping hill. There is a tall floor lamp by the chair, but the light is not on—no need. Our newspaper comes in the afternoon; Mom gathers me, her three-year-old daughter, into her lap and holds me closely, snuggled into a peaceful lull. She reads me the comic strips from the newspaper. I can hear my mother breathing as she rocks and clutches me close to her, and then we laugh at the latest escapades of Beetle Bailey. The silent air again is broken with our laughter as Dagwood outwits Blondie or Mr. Dithers, Nancy and Sluggo get into benign mischief, or a doctor and nurse save a life from a dreaded but little-known disease. Now I don't remember the names of the fictional doctor-nurse characters, but perhaps they reminded my mom of her days—just four or five years before—at the hospital where she had been head nurse.

I sometimes wonder now how she felt about going from that thriving hospital nurses' station that she commanded during and just after World War II to that quiet rocker in the farm house on the rich green hill at the city limits of a hamlet of a few hundred people—only seventeen miles away, but a world from her career. She must have embodied some remorse about walking away from her profession—at least from time to time. After all, I—her captivated, awed child audience smiling up at her in that cocoon rocker as she read—could not comprehend the demands on a woman in the 1940s and 1950s whose aspirations to be a doctor were crushed by the financial and cultural limits of the day.

In the years to come, I would sometimes see her get a faraway look in her eyes when she would recount again how she literally had her suitcase packed after applying to be a Navy nurse in WWII—an appointment with potential for medical school. Then, she would lovingly look at me and explain—for me or herself, I don't know—how the doctor in charge of the hospital dashed her hopes when he offhandedly commented that she wasn't going to the Navy for she had been deemed "essential" to the medical needs of this rural West Tennessee region. Then, Mom's voice would become almost a whisper as she would tell me how she unpacked and went back to the daily hospital routine.

As I look back now, I have a deeper appreciation of the longing she had to be a doctor, and it was Mom's medical acumen that the St. Jude's doctors recognized and that drew them to turn to her objective questions rather than my hope-gorged ones. Even today, personally, I gag at the sight of blood and offer only sympathy when treatment would be the desired response.

Whatever Mom felt about giving up her nursing profession, she never shared in depth with me as a small child, in fact, never shared throughout her life. Now, in her silence I will never know. But I do know that she was my first teacher, enticing me with the exciting world of reading in that rocking chair cocoon and offering me an invitation to join her in that world which would present both of us opportunities for encouragement and escape (Wright 211-212).

Chapter 13

My Transition

It would be several years in school before I would again accept that intimacy of the world of reading Mom offered. First grade was tolerable, maybe at times fun, but by second grade I had realized this school thing was not a short-lived routine. There would be a drought of second and third grades when I would cry because I had to go to school. I would often "feel sick" and have to go to the principal's office to call home for Mom to pick me up. I would start feeling ill when I would get out my "box" to do coloring, cutting, and drawing. My cherished "box" was a cardboard cigar box with a flip top that we got at the local grocery when all of its contents had been emptied by the cigar-smokers of my small town. Regardless of its earlier contents, it contained my treasures—my mom's surgery scissors from the hospital, paper dolls that she and I had cut out, colors that were usually well-worn from home projects, all mementos that made me long for the security of her voice, her laughter, her lap.

Mom understood and weathered my clinging arms. But after weeks of frustration with my crying and begging not to go to school during second grade, Dad calmly declared that he was going to "switch" my legs all the way up the long foreboding school sidewalk—in front of all of the children—if I did not assume my place in the classroom. As miserable as I was, I couldn't bear the thought of the other kids laughing at me, so I never again protested. I thought that no one at school, not even the teacher, realized just how miserable I was. Only in later years, when I was an adult would Mom reveal to me that the second-grade teacher had confided at a parent-teacher conference, "I think Jenna just doesn't like me!"

In her wisdom, Mom didn't respond but changed the subject. Ironically, years after Mom's death I saw this teacher at a local hometown restaurant. Although she was well into her nineties, she looked the same she did to me as a seven-year-old. When she saw me, she broke into a warm smile. She seemed to be pleased to see me. She even ranted on what a fine student I had been so many years ago. She thanked me for remembering her and coming over to speak to her. She never let on a minute that she remembered what I was really like in that second-grade classroom. Mom's earlier discretion at the parent-teacher conference had paid off.

Later, being a university professor, I confess that I feel bad that I didn't like my teacher—but it wasn't her fault. Remembering how I felt as a seven-year-old, I believe that I longed to hear my mother's breathing as she read and we laughed—not the voice of a stranger sharing those cherished moments with twenty other children ready to lie on plastic padded mats placed methodically on cold gray tile floors. There was little pleasure there in second-grade reading—the culmination of laughter and snuggles with Mom was replaced by a culmination of workbook activities demanding coloring, circles, and "right" answers. Mom never insisted on "right" answers after our readings. In fact, there were no questions.

Each fall when school begins, I am reminded that I never had the opportunity to read to Mandy, to plant the joy of learning, or to take her to her first day at school.

When our son, Zac, two years younger than Mandy, went to his first day at kindergarten, another mother called me to commiserate on her grief that her son, too, had left her "nest" to start school that day.

"I called you because I knew you would understand since you and Zac are so close," she said. Then she stopped talking because her voice broke into sobs.

I said nothing.

She snubbed and sniffed. "I know you must be just as sad as I am."

"No . . . no," I said.

"Of course . . . you are probably sadder." She had stopped crying.

"Actually, I'm happy. Two years ago, I wanted to take Mandy to kindergarten, but school started without her. It was a joy to walk Zac to his class today."

"Oh . . . " she said.

I heard the phone click.

She and I never were close friends.

Now, I wonder if Mandy would have liked school . . . if she would have been studious, athletic, popular.

I wonder who she was.

Chapter 14

Mama's Baby: Daddy's Maybe

As a child, I never realized the influence Mom had on me in both a patriarchal family and a patriarchal Southern culture. I was Daddy's girl. In fact, Dad and I, in my mind, took care of Mom. It was a long time before I realized I, too, was supposed to be of the weaker sex. Since there were no sons, to me, I embodied both son and daughter expectations.

When playing with dolls as a nine-year-old, I would often pretend that I was on a wagon train going out West and that I had three dolls as my children. My husband was an invalid in the wagon, and I took care of my family, making all of the decisions. (Today, I wonder what a therapist would make of this play scenario.) I can still see the two-foot tall child's red rocker where the dolls sat as I drove the wagon into the unexplored West. Admittedly, I was influenced by the weekly television western that my family watched, *Wagon Train*. But on that show, Major Adams, leader of the wagon train, and Flint, the train's scout, embodied the ultimate macho male. The women were for the most part weak and dependent on the male who was taking them out West, as well as on the wagon train staff who were all males. So, why did I aspire to have my family on a train with a weak husband in the wagon so that I could care for him and lead our family to the promised land of the Old West?

Probably, the inspiration was from both Dad and Mom. Dad, because he wanted strength in the family for the future, and because of medical reasons, there would be no sons, in fact, no more children after me. Mom, because she had experienced the strength in her mom while the family struggled financially during the Great Depression. But for many years, whatever the reasons and whoever the family author, I only saw that I was Daddy's girl, emanating his strength.

A few years ago, an incident at the local hair salon started me to thinking about how our family was a clandestine haven of matriarchal inspiration and power. Not long after our son, Zac, had completed a study abroad in Edinburgh, Scotland, I was having my hair styled and was talking about his educational experience abroad. Several clients and stylists began asking questions about the culture there in Edinburgh—food, clothing, housing. One particular client getting her haircut asked if he purchased and/or wore kilts while he was there in Celtic country.

Explaining that my husband's family had a rich Scottish history through the Haliburton clan of Scotland—the grandmother of Sir Walter Scott, famous Scottish writer and statesman, was a member of the Haliburton clan—I concluded with the story of Zac's order for a kilt at a tailor's shop on the Royal Mile. The tailor went through scans of materials to determine the tartan that represented my husband and son's family heritage—both the Haliburton name and the Dryburgh Abbey hometown area. I crowned my Great Britain story with the jewel that the kilt was quite expensive—over $500—but has continued to be a precious memento of Zac's time in Scotland.

The wife of a local doctor who had been listening closely and had contributed her roots from the Scots looked perplexed as I was explaining the significance of family and place to others there caught in the conquest of beauty among the tin foils, highlights, lowlights, clippers, and Aveda all-naturals.

Finally, she spoke, "You know—your son's tartan was not correctly chosen. He followed the line of his father—albeit from his father's grandmother. The tartan must follow the Scottish line from the mother."

She saw my surprise. After all, the tailor in Edinburgh had never mentioned such a requirement as he figured the cost in British pounds. (Scottish pounds would have been a better exchange for the American dollar at the time.)

Her triumphant declaration split the air in that beauty shop like the scissors on the long strands of the cascading blond locks of an elementary school girl sitting in the chair across the aisle from me.

"After all," the physician's mate alleged, "Mother's baby; Father's maybe."

The whole salon erupted in laughter, including the male stylist on my color.

"No, really," she said. "That is right! You certainly belong to your mother; therefore, the tartan—your heritage—must come through the female line of the family."

I've thought about her words from time to time. Oh, not a question of a child's physical paternity, but rather a question of a parent's influence . . . Is a child mostly the mother's baby?

As I pondered the answer to that question in my own heritage, I thought back and remembered some events in my more formative years.

Dad used to ask me in a child's question-answer game mode, "Who do you love the most in all of the world?"

He always asked me that question in a group of friends or relatives, and my four-year-old mouth would proudly proclaim the words he longed to hear or maybe needed to hear in and among those particular people who were listening.

"I love my daddy!" I would shout—for surely the loudness would prove my point. I sometimes appropriately whined out the words stretching them as long as breath and intonation could stand. I might run up and hug and kiss Daddy. I'd ignore Mom, standing nearby with her soft smile. Sometimes, I'd look at her with a slighted love and a smirk that would underscore the intensity and veracity of my testimony of comparative love. After all, why would anyone think there would or could be a different answer? I was the insatiable "Daddy's girl" at that young age.

The relatives and friends would smile and wink at Daddy, but Mom didn't flinch—ever present, ever gracious, ever the buffer in this children's game.

And then the follow-up question evoked more of a child's protestation, "Whose girl are you?"

"Daddy's!" I elongated the declaration as though I would receive a trophy for each musical syllable.

"No, you're not; you're Mama's girl," he would challenge—just to rile my minion spirit.

"I am not!" I would protest.

But today my spirit and my mouth confirm, "Yes, I am Mama's girl!"

PENSIVE NOW, I am ever reminded that although I am greatly blessed, I will never raise a Mama's girl. But . . . I will always rejoice in being a Mama's girl!

Chapter 15

An Opal

And I was never more her girl than when I stood before Mom's casket at the church only minutes before I would see her no more. Mrs. Jozelle, my high school Sunday school teacher, hugged me and whispered consoling words.

"Virginia loved you so much. Always remember you never brought a tear to your mom's eyes." Mrs. Jozelle's kind smile and soft eyes reflected her loving heart.

What comfort! Yes, some mothers spent many nights weeping over something their children had done. This assurance that I had spared Mom that hurt in life should have been a comfort. But Mrs. Jozelle didn't know . . .

DURING MY CHILDHOOD, Mom always had her most prized jewelry in a small red jewelry box outlined in gold that rested in the top drawer of her dresser. What delight it brought me as a child to be privy to her earrings, necklaces, and bracelets when playing dress-up. In that game, often I would wear her old nurse's uniform. I never remember wearing her nurse's hat with its braid and pins, but I remember the once stiff and starched white uniform that had a few years before tightly belted Mom's ninety-two pound body. Now it caressed my gangly body caring for imaginary patients in the front yard of our pink PermaStone house. Then after my shift at the front-yard hospital would end, I would find great joy in wearing Mom's stylish dresses, which I often took from her wardrobe in the back bedroom closet.

I was a fine sight in the wide brim or pillbox hats with the flowing strands of pearls, colored beads, or 14K gold convoluted chains clutching my neck. The earrings were my favorite—large round, shinny purple bobs with a raised glowing center or yellow and green sunburst orbs that clipped onto earlobes and caused them to droop like the tired, sagging breasts of an aged, wrinkled grandmother. Those earrings were often gifts from the glass jewelry counters of the local drug store where on birthdays, anniversaries, and Christmas for $1.13 Daddy and I would make our purchases. Mrs. Lucille, the druggist's wife and the Sunday school teacher for the Golden Circle Class, Mom's class, would help us choose just what she would like.

Then there were the chunky bracelets, which often came with the more expensive jewelry sets—$2.26 for a matching bracelet to really make the gift special. I loved to coordinate Mom's dresses hanging loosely on my child body with the bracelets slipping carelessly on and off over my petite wrists.

I was a sight, a miniature Mom I thought. But I never wore her rings. Mom had her wedding band, a plain gold circle with a few tiny diamonds that would—when Daddy became more prosperous—be replaced by six large diamonds surrounded with fourteen baguettes. And the other ring in her jewelry box had a small slip-top container all its own, placed there carefully years before never to be disturbed.

It was a large multi-faceted opal with two small diamonds on each side. A yellow gold band carried this ring that became a quest for me. Mom told me the opal was the birthstone for her October birthday. Mine was the deep red garnet for January, and it paled in sight of the miraculously formed opal.

I just had to wear that ring, just one time, for my friends at school to see its beauty—to see my mother's never-worn treasure kept in a box within a box in a drawer in her bedroom.

I don't know why she ever agreed to my wearing that ring to school. Perhaps she wanted to share its beauty. Perhaps she thought at that particular time my child ego needed the boost of the "oos" and "ahs" of other little girls in my small rural classroom. Perhaps she just tired of my begging and on the spur of the moment gave in. Whatever the reason, I donned that lovely ring on my tiny hand after Mom wrapped white tape around its back to secure it to my finger for the day.

Oh, how the other girls did marvel at my ring that day on the playground as we ran and played and ate our recess snacks.

It wasn't until I was putting on my coat that afternoon that I looked down at the treasure that had brought me so much joy that day and discovered the opal was missing. The diamonds gleamed beside the open hole revealing the gorge of skin on my finger where the opal stone once stood.

When she came to pick me up after school, I ran to the car to tell Mom of the loss. She drove home in silence. After my daily ritual of Coke and a candy bar at the kitchen table, I found her crying in her and Dad's bedroom. I had never seen her cry before.

She and I went back to the playground and searched for the stone; she called my teacher, and an alert for the opal was sent around the halls of the elementary school the next day. But no one ever found the opal that had brought Mom—and me—so much pleasure.

Years later I would learn of a young man Mom knew long before she met Dad, a young man who died in his early twenties, a young man who had wanted to marry her. I discovered that the opal ring had been a gift from him.

After I lost the opal, Mom put a garnet stone in the setting surrounded by the diamonds and gave the ring as a gift to me when I graduated from elementary to junior high. But the ring would never again bring me pleasure. When I looked at it, I saw a garnet trying to take the place of an opal—a gem more valuable, more beautiful, more multifaceted, more precious than a garnet. A garnet could not replace an opal in that diamond setting. I could never replace, nor would I desire to replace, Mom in any setting. She was my mom, and in many ways in the rural South of the 1940s and later . . . a woman before her time! A woman who had a successful career as a nurse and stayed single by choice until she was 32 years old but a woman whose goal to be a doctor was thwarted by the place of women in the rural South and the socio-economic times of the WWII era!

Chapter 16

"Virginia" Moments

Like the opal, Mom was multifaceted, but no facet was as endearing as her naivety to make me and others laugh—the "Virginia" moments we called them. She—who was revered by her patients, who ran a three-floor hospital as head nurse during the tumultuous days of World War II; she—with all of her intelligence, education, efficiency, and effectiveness! She had a complexity of innocence and naivety that could bring those around her to tears of laughter.

I remember when as a first-year college student I went with Mom and my cousin Dot over to a clothing outlet at Cookeville. Dad drove us over the curvy mountainous road around by the scenic overlook at Center Hill Lake and onto busy Interstate 40—all so we could buy beautiful slacks, sweaters, and dresses at discount prices from a factory outlet.

When we arrived at the large vinyl building found at the edge of the city, Dad made known his plans to stay in the car at best or at worst to stand in the steamy sunshine heat on that summer day where the thick trees tried to shade the outlet.

I can just see Dad in his small-brimmed dressy summer hat,

white tipped cigar in his mouth, tan putter pants, and khaki plaid short-sleeved shirt. Waiting outside of or beside the car, he would talk with other husbands, fathers, or boyfriends, all exiled to this gravel outpost that hosted a harem of female shoppers.

Dressed in her stylish yellow pants suit and silver hoop earrings, Mom, as usual, determined early in the scouting period that she surely didn't need anything and that there were several really cute outfits that I should try on. Thousands upon thousands of hangers displaying colorful garments contrasted and coordinated for the shopping eye, but none pleased her that day. I must say that several years later after I was married, I realized just how Mom's taste in clothes had appreciated and the price of her clothes had simultaneously escalated. When she deleted my clothing allowance, she had obviously found a new source of revenue.

But at the outlet that day, my clothes were still the largest expenditures in her clothing line items, so I gathered five or six outfits—sweaters, slacks, shirts, shorts—and went into a massive dressing arena.

There I found twelve or fifteen individual dressing rooms five feet by eight feet with curtained rods to protect privacy and mirrors to reflect the appropriate view of the latest selection. At the north end of these linear, clustered dressing rooms was a large "foyer" area complete with attractive built-in wooden oak benches lining the east side of the wall directly across from a wall of mirrors. The triad of mirrors allowed each shopper the opportunity to see the latest fashion from all angles.

Most of the dressing rooms were in use by frugal shoppers. Sitting on the bench, Mom and Dot were caught in conversation that was interrupted from time to time by their laughter or the laughter of another spectator shopper.

After trying on and eliminating one or two of my potential buys there in my dressing room, I put on an above-the-knee summer skirt and matching cotton pull-over in a melon orange that I thought earned a second look at the mirrors in the larger dressing room and an evaluation by Mom and Dot.

As I moved like a New York runway model across the cluttered outlet floor to give the full effect of what this matched skirt and top could do for my 103-pound, 5-foot–6-inch frame, I couldn't even get the two of them to glance up at me.

Dot in her professional navy business suit with its white under-blouse was laughing so hard she was almost shaking the built-in bench.

And Mom, with a stunned look on her face and a mouth paused to burst into uncontrollable laughter as soon as the initial shock wore off, looked up to see me approaching. In the flurry of other shoppers surveying their clothes in the mirrors, I sat down on the bench next to Dot. As soon as she could get her breath and keep her voice low enough that others would not hear, she began to recount the incident that had brought her to laughing tears.

It seemed that the two of them had been quietly discussing where we would have lunch when Mom noticed one large middle-aged woman standing almost in front of the two of them. She turned from side to side at the wall of mirrors where she was evaluating her soft mint green dress with price tags begrudgingly hanging from under her arm.

Mom looked up and in a spirit of good-natured friendliness and compliments pointed to the woman who was now walking back to the dressing room. In a voice louder than Mom and Dot had been using in their lunch-plan conversation but still a soft Southern drawl, Mom declared, "Oh, you must buy that dress. It fits you well and compliments the color of your hair and your skin tone."

As the woman turned to look at her complimenter face-to-face, Mom added convincingly, "unlike that blue one you had on a minute ago. Don't buy that blue one—it doesn't do a thing for you."

Abashed, the woman looked back at her reflection in the distant mirrors across the room and then turned from the mirrors to face Mom and Dot. "Well! I've never . . . that blue dress is the one I wore into this store! It is <u>my</u> dress!"

With that declaration she huffed back into the confinement and security of her five-by-eight dressing room—leaving Mom to face the laughter of Dot and the entire bevy of would-be buyers in the forest of mirrors.

I have thought of this encounter at the dress outlet many times—in fact, I wrote a terse version—100 to 150 words only—for one of the $100 reader-entry sections of *Reader's Digest*. But —to no avail. Maybe I just couldn't do it justice in my retelling.

Recently, in thinking about Mom and her ability to naively bring a friend, a family member, or even a room full of strangers to laughter, I realized one principle she lived by. I can honestly say I never saw her intentionally hurt anyone with her humor—in fact, most of the time her own ego was the one that hung in the balance. But, her kind spirit and soft demeanor somehow brought to her an endearment that permeated those who knew her or had the privilege for a once-in-a-lifetime meeting—although I am not so sure the lady who left the outlet that day in her own blue dress would agree with me!

Mom could never live down another "Virginia" moment—a family story that reverberated through many family dinners, especially in the summer at July 4th gatherings where we would feast on Dad's grilled steaks and homemade banana ice cream. Often at the end of that holiday meal, the Texas vacation story became the second dessert.

I loved the summer vacations that Mom and Dad would plan for us—beginning with early wake-up calls, sometimes as early as 2:00 a.m. because Dad wanted to travel in the early mornings before daylight. Those early hours allowed faster (fewer cars and trucks on the numerous two-lane highways of the day) and cooler (few cars with air conditioning then) travel. Dad, always the pilot of our car, wanted Mom to be his navigator—the map-reader, an assignment for which she had no talent. She sported absolutely no sense of direction.

I remember during my teen-age years a summer vacation in Texas in the heat of mid-July. As I read my book in the back seat of the car, I vaguely listened to Dad's concern about whether he was on the right highway or not. Finally in desperation and nearing a place he could turn around, Dad asked Mom to watch for a sign identifying the highway we were traveling.

A few minutes later, Mom gasped and screamed, "Stop, stop! Turn around! We are on 55 and 65."

When Dad hit the brakes to quickly turn, he spotted the 55 and 65 sign—identifying the speed limit!

He shouted his frustration as he verbally challenged Mom's intelligence—she the head surgical nurse at a hospital. But, she calmly explained that steering through the abdomen or the chest cavity was not the same as maneuvering through the highways and byways of the great Lone Star state of Texas!

I wonder now if Mom was ever really embarrassed by these "Virginia" moments or the laughter they evoked in their frequent retelling, but I never asked and she never shared. Sometimes when my family laughs at me in my "Virginia" moments, I do wonder!

Chapter 17

Cokes

In the South, it is common knowledge that any carbonated drink is often called Coke. It can be Dr. Pepper, R.C., or even Pepsi—but if it is a dark carbonated beverage, it is a Coke. From childhood, Mom never liked water. Her younger sister, Frances, was the water drinker. It was a family joke that if the house caught on fire, Aunt Frances would have to stop and get a drink of water before escaping the disaster. But not Mom. She didn't like the taste of water; she didn't drink water.

Cokes were the drink of choice in Mom's life. She had depended on the caffeine to help her stay awake on the eleven-to-seven shift when she was a young nurse in training, and they became a constant companion for life. She only left Cokes when Diet Cokes came out.

Mom had a Coke every morning before breakfast, nursed one or two all day long, and then had one more before going to bed.

While shopping at a supermarket in a neighboring town, Mom and Dad stopped at a taste-test table being sponsored by Pepsi. By this time in her life, Mom had been drinking Cokes for fifty years.

"Just taste these two drinks and tell me which is better." The young man behind the table was eager for a taster.

Mom sipped on the first one, and then turned her taste buds to the second. After finishing off both drinks, she said, "No question about it. This is the better drink—the Coke." The young man at the tasting table smiled and with a rising voice declared for others to hear, "Yes, mam! That's right. You have chosen the Pepsi!"

"I did not," Mom said.

"Yes, mam . . . see this is the Pepsi." He pointed to the number on her cup and the number showing on the card. Sure enough, there was the word PEPSI.

"I don't care—Coke is better anyway!"

Mom pushed her buggy on to the next aisle with little fluster . . . at least little fluster on her part.

Taste testing had no significance. She had a lifetime of Coke, and no brief encounter with Pepsi would change that.

In her later years when her health began to fail, she would sit in the blue den recliner with the daily newspaper near on the floor, the fireplace burning, one of her favorite game shows filling the TV screen, and she would sip on her Diet Coke—not the green glass bottled Coke from the past, but a glass of Coke from a two-liter plastic, a cheaper Coke product but the same great taste.

Perhaps it was her obsession with Diet Coke that made her last few days in congestive heart failure both devastating and ironical.

She was drowning in her own fluid. The doctors told us they were at the maximum level of diuretics.

The order was that she could have no liquids unless approved by the nursing staff. It was a losing battle. She was so thirsty, but liquids only added to the fluids that were drowning her. Dad and I were cautioned about even a spoonful of ice placed behind her parched lips.

As her birthday approached, her friends were organizing a mass birthday card effort. I asked Mom one morning as she lay hooked to tubes surrounding her hospital bed, "What do you want for your birthday?"

She didn't even have to think. "A glass of ice water."

I had to leave the room.

Chapter 18

Mom's Apology

Mom didn't apologize much—didn't have to very often. And she was gracious in accepting apologies. So when she confessed she owed me an apology—I was in my thirties at the time—I was intrigued.

My father's family was and is very musical. His oldest sibling, a sister, played the mandolin, his oldest brother the banjo, his youngest brother the piano and accordion, and my dad the guitar. All four children sang beautifully. My grandmother played the guitar and piano, and both of my grandparents sang. My great-grandfather was a music teacher by profession. Music was at the core of my dad's home life although neither parent earned money with music.

That place of money for music was, however, more viable for the lives of both my dad and his youngest brother. Dad played in a band in the years just before WWII. In fact, he was with a band when he went into the Army where he would eventually become a WWII disabled veteran. After the war, Dad went to school on the GI bill, farmed, and eventually became a successful real estate broker in his home county. His music after the war was limited to singing as choir director and often doing special music for church services and funerals.

My Uncle Gordon Stoker, on the other hand, left a job as pianist for the John Daniel Quartet to serve in WWII and returned from service in the Army Air Corp to later become a renowned member of the Jordanaires Quartet that backed such famous stars as Elvis Presley, Ricky Nelson, and Patsy Cline, and the star list continues.

In fact, when I was a small child, the Jordanaires needed a bass singer, and my uncle asked Dad if he would be interested in joining the group. But he was not inclined to the rigorous appearance schedule and long sessions, so he declined the offer—saying he liked to hunt and fish at will.

When I look back on his decision, I wonder how my mother felt. My dad, a small Southern rural real estate broker, made a good living, but nothing to even remotely compare to what he would have made as a member of the Jordanaires. There would have been opportunities for travel and for a big-city environment that would have offered larger hospitals and the possibility of more medical training for Mom.

I never remember my mother giving an opinion on this invitation, and I have heard her recount the story of the invitation with no implications of regret. I used to wonder why she would not have resented his turning down "fame and fortune" as it were. That is until the apology.

As a child I loved to sing. I had a good memory and knew the words to most songs introduced in my musical environment. I took piano lessons from Miss Reba, the teacher of my uncle, a child prodigy. At the age of three after attending a gospel music concert, he came home, climbed on the piano bench, and, to the delight of my grandparents, played one of the songs from the evening—played it "by ear."

On the other hand, I had no innate musical ability, which at the age of eight came to my attention as I attempted a duet for a Christmas program.

After the church service, we were at my grandparents' home, and I asked my grandfather how I did. He hugged me and said, "Just fine. Just fine."

My grandfather was the love of my life as a child, and being the only grandchild in the same town with him, we were very close. He was a kind, good man.

Only a few years ago at a writing conference, I ran into a teacher/writer who had grown up in the same church with me. She began reminiscing about my deacon grandfather. She asked me if I remembered how he always closed his public prayers in the church services. Both of us said at the same time, "Let us overcome evil with good."

And he lived his life in that challenge. Perhaps that's why he told me my singing was "just fine." He was overcoming with good.

But later that night, my dad would confess to me that I was off-key throughout the entire Christmas carol—although my friend had carried the tune "just fine."

After that embarrassment, my mother got me some "sing-along" records for children. And although by then my dad had asked her to never sing with me—she had a tin ear—she encouraged me to practice with the children on the records. It would be much later after years of piano and voice lessons that I would be able to "carry a tune."

At thirty and in tune enough to sing in a choir, I listened to Mom's apology.

It seems that when Mom first married, it was common for Dad's parents and siblings to sing at family get-togethers. As a new bride, Mom loved being a part of the talented musicians gathered in my grandparents' living room. But she had not been a part of the family very long when at the end of a song, my grandmother made fun of Mom's out-of-tune rendition. Whether an intentional hurt or not, Mom was hurt, and she never sang again at the family musicals. She was always the audience.

WHEN I WAS A BABY, Mom asked God not to give me my dad's family's musical talent. She feared the musical ability would take me away from her. For thirty years she carried that secret and guilt while watching me struggle to be musical.

Mom was never close to her mother-in-law, but, as a nurse, served as Grandmother's primary healthcare giver until her death. Mom could do that because she had forgiven my grandmother... who never knew she needed forgiveness.

I accepted Mom's apology.

I never heard Mandy sing, but she loved music, even her doctor's French lullabies at St. Jude's Hospital when her life was fleeting. It was one of the things that brought her happiness.

I believe that both Mom and Mandy are singing now with perfect pitch and rhythm—singing of forgiveness far beyond what Mom and I understood at the time.

"Grace amazing,

Grace unfailing

Grace that saves my soul"

From "Grace That Won't Let Go" by Thomas Miller and Mark Harris

Chapter 19
My Apology

I wonder sometimes how Mom and I could be so close and yet so different. Mom's scientific nursing approach to life and my humanities English approach were not always conducive to each other and to us. But, I must admit that as a child I loved the prestige of my mother being "the nurse" in a town that sometimes had no doctor practicing there. Calls from neighbors and friends with medical questions were always treated with respect, and one of Mom's responses culminated in a woman's life-saving cancer surgery—just because of Mom's recognition of symptoms.

She not only helped save lives because of her expertise but also offered dignity in the final days of life for some. More than once, she served as a hospice nurse and encouraged and comforted both patients and families.

In her mid-thirties, and no longer head nurse at her beloved hospital seventeen miles away, she was revered in this small, rural town where she settled and made her home for over 46 years.

As her child, I enjoyed the privileges of having a mom who knew how to treat children's illnesses—mumps, measles, whooping cough, chicken pox—all of which I became the recipient. But, she always knew what to do—unlike the mothers of many of my friends who had to call her. And, Mom always had the "pull" to get me into the doctor's office in the neighboring town when others might have to wait for an appointment. But with all of those perks came the division of different spirits—one whose head led and one whose heart led.

I suppose the most prominent memory of such a clash of spirits was when Mandy was terminally ill at St. Jude's Hospital in Memphis. Mom sought the scientific answers—symptoms, protocol, prognosis. And I, well, I sought the human—no pain, restored life, hope. The two were never that far apart in the final analysis—but so far apart in the application.

The questions she asked the doctor were so detached, so factual. How could she be so aloof in her conversation with him? Yet, he seemed to be so much more comfortable with her questions than mine. The two of them had been trained to move into a mode that made them effective in helping others—an objectivity that kept them from being so sympathetic and empathetic that they could not function medically.

I, on the other hand, could not go there—to a land void of feelings.

I never told Mom, but I wish I had: I'm glad she was able to be that person in the family for Mandy. At the time, I was upset with Mom for not being and feeling just like me. But, Mandy needed the ability Mom had to understand and interpret the doctor's unspoken messages.

Unlike her, I could not move in that realm of objectivity—not even for Mom herself in the last days. The doctor told me she was dying weeks before she did. I denied it. I couldn't accept it—holding out hope until I saw her breathe her last breath to join Mandy who was waiting.

In the later years of Mom's life, I was full-time English

faculty at the University of Tennessee at Martin. During her frequent hospital stays, I would teach my classes and then travel to the hospital where she was—whether Martin, Jackson, or Memphis.

That last day, the chair of my department came to my class and told me to dismiss the students and join my dad at the hospital in Memphis because my mom needed me. When I arrived at the hospital in Memphis, I told Mom I had finished my morning class before Earl and I came down. Fighting for oxygen through the mask in these last stages of congestive heart failure, she looked at me and said, "Enjoy your work!"

I've thought about the admonition many times since that day. It was the last of much advice that she gave me. I've wondered if she regretted leaving the medical profession to raise me. Ironically, the profession never left her. That approach was a problem for me, her humanities child.

I remember that after Mandy died Mom tried to raise my depressed spirit with her scientific stance emerging again; she told me that it was better Mandy than I. She said that I could have other children right away. I was crushed; didn't she love Mandy as I did?

I was furious with Mom—until a friend of hers with whom I was sharing this hurt responded, "She feels the same way you do; you are her child just as Mandy was your child. You are to her as Mandy is to you."

I never told Mom how angry her remark had made me, so I never told her I finally understood. Maybe some things are better never spoken.

After Mom died, my aunt shared with me what Mom had written her following Mandy's death.

I never saw the letter, but supposedly it went something like this:

Jenna Stoker Wright

My dear Frances,

Thank you for the beautiful flowers you sent for Mandy's funeral. The spray of yellow roses with baby's breath was a sweet reminder of your love.

I know you wanted to come to be near us as we went through this heartbreak, but you didn't need to make that six-hundred-mile drive with your leg problems.

Jenna is really having a hard time, and the Christmas season is not encouraging. Past and planned happiness invades the despair she feels and only heightens it.

I feel so helpless in trying to comfort her—I find myself telling her these things happen, and she must move on. She just continues to weep and looks past me in a blank stare—or worse screams that I don't understand how she feels.

And she's right—I don't.

By the way, don't worry about having to convince my family to take me to Eastside. They buried Mandy there, so we purchased our plots to be buried near her. Now I don't have to worry about where I will be buried—I can have final rest back in my hometown.

Come when you are better. We can talk about all that has happened.

Your sister,
Virginia

Even in her reflections on Mandy's death, Mom found an objectivity I could not. I just wasn't a protégé of Mom's sciences. Our son, Zac, used to say he could bleed to death while I sympathized with him assuring him I knew it hurt. His dad was the emergency nurse—I the long-sleepless-nights-and-high-fever nurse. But although I wasn't her protégé, I think I found in her last days the mettle Mom had always wondered if I had. Now, I wonder if she was really alert enough—on the morphine—to know.

Only a few hours before Mom would leave us, a surgical nurse sent up to the room asked one family member to stay with her as she tried to insert an IV tube into a vein near Mom's heart. Other veins had now collapsed.

Surprisingly, Dad, who prided himself in his ability to handle these situations better than I, said he just couldn't do it. In all fairness, he was much better in those situations than I. But not that day. So, I said I would stay. I realize now the nurses knew the end was very near and keeping family nearby was calming for Mom. I'm sure she recognized all of these impending death symptoms, but I did not.

I stood and held Mom's hand and talked with her about . . . I don't know what! And then, the nurse had the IV in, and she was leaving us. For that few minutes, my inability to deal with medical objectivity had been cauterized, and I was Mom's child—if only in the last hours of her life.

I owed Mom an apology. There was room for both of our personalities in Mandy's life and death. Not just room, there was a need for both of us. I had years to apologize to Mom, but unlike the wisdom she found to share, I never did. Somehow, I like to think she knew I came to peace with our differences. There was no question she knew I loved her!

Chapter 20

The Golden Circle

The Golden Circle—that's what Mom's Bible study class was called. I didn't know until her funeral that she was a founding member.

There her class sat together as honorary pallbearers. Many of the women by then were in their sixties and seventies, but that class had begun as a group of young wives and mothers in a Southern Baptist Church in the late 1940s. At that time in our small Southern Baptist congregation, women were called on to lead in prayer in the worship services and led in many of the outreach ministries. I do not know if these leadership roles reflected our individual church's doctrine or were related to the experiences of WWII and the population of men at home, but still in my childhood of the 1950s, these leadership roles continued and have always broadened my view of women's roles in the church. Many of the tenets of individual church autonomy were impacted by the Southern Baptist Convention during those forty or more years of the Golden Circle's existence, but the autonomy of the women in that class never changed. That band of like believers was Mom's support group throughout her life.

The teacher from the early inception of the class of fifteen women was the local pharmacist's wife—she herself not a native of the town. Class members hailed from as far away as the state of Virginia. Only a few of the group were still in their hometown. Perhaps that fact coupled with Mom's early religious training of weekly church services drew her to these women. They were truly major in her life in a town where she never seemed to feel she quite "fit." But she "fit" with these women—many who worked outside the home in their husband's businesses, the town's clothing factories, or their own businesses (usually a local beauty shop or what we would call today a hair salon).

This circle of friends was a mainstay in Mom's life. Once a month, they met in a member's home for a class meeting with a business session—determining benevolent projects for the next month, hearing a treasurer's report, giving an offering brought by each member. Then there would be a devotion, a time of prayer for the needs of the members and those they knew, a game related to the month's holiday or Bible study, and refreshments. Refreshments were usually a full meal.

Mom delighted in these meetings. Even after I moved away and married, she would call to regale the food, the games, and the gossip. Gossip was always termed as news, and sometimes as prayer requests.

As a girl, I regarded these women as friendship models—varying education levels, varying financial levels, varying professional levels. They were bound together by living in the South at a time when the roles of women were changing. Few of these women were college graduates although as the class grew in later years, there were degree-holding members, but few in my childhood and teenage years.

These women knew who they were and set the stage for their children to go beyond the expectations of a small Southern town. Many of their children would be first-generation college students.

This circle of friends shared not only their joys and sorrows but also the "in's" and "out's" of their marriages—the foibles of husbands too.

One class member confided in Mom over the 4-digit phone—our number was 2881, I still remember—that her husband had been frantic that particular morning looking for his favorite ball cap. He was planning to return after his day at work to "tear up" the closet looking for that cap. But she knew that his search was futile. Only to Mom would she confess that she had burned the cap in the trash the day before after months of trying to get him to throw it away.

These were the whispers, the giggles, the confidences that as a child I would hear as I walked through our dining room where the small phone stand was placed beside a dining table chair. There Mom would sit and "visit"—no texting, no email, no Facebook—just a landline phone.

At times my trust in Mom's integrity was challenged when I would hear her confide something with the caveat that this juicy tidbit was a hush-hush—not to be told—because Dad had shared it in confidence. Mom would hang up the phone in total assurance that her dear friend would keep the secret.

Sometimes it was necessary to keep a secret from another member of the circle, and those times were taken very seriously. In fact, the major reason to do so often involved not hurting the other circle member.

Such was a time when three of the circle were traveling to shop in a neighboring town. Sitting in the backseat of the car and hearing the front-seaters recounting the latest skirmishes with their husbands—all of which were minor since both marriages would last forty plus years—the listening woman declared what she believed to be the strength of her marriage.

"My husband and I never have had an argument in all of our married life," she interjected into the conversation.

No front-seater responded to her declaration. After separating from her in the first store visit, Mom and the other front-seater could hardly contain themselves.

"Of course, they have never had an argument," Mom said. "She has never challenged a thing he ever said."

Mom never planned to commit to that kind of relationship because she would later tell me, "If there are no disagreements in a marriage, there is an imbalance of power. One person is powerful; one is powerless."

According to Mom, the subject of marriage disagreements was never again broached with the friend. After all, she was a part of the circle—the golden circle. Even though they doubted her strength to stand up for herself, they knew that her strength in the circle came from the bond that was there and that each member needed that strength.

This Rosie-the-Riveter circle of women often found a juxtaposition of social, economic, and political values in light of deep conservative Southern Baptist principles. The circles' politics was mixed with Democrats and Republicans and Independents. Mom was a "yellow dog" Democrat—she would vote for a yellow dog if it appeared on the Democratic ticket. Once when her better judgment would not allow her to vote Democratic, she refused that day to go to the voting polls with Dad, who was raised in a Republican home, voted for the person not the party, and did not often talk politics because it hurt business.

During the 1960 Presidential election, our pastor had an altar call for prayer about the upcoming vote. According to him, the Catholic John F. Kennedy was running and would be the nemesis of Protestants in America. Mom was furious with that theory and let her thoughts be known in the circle. Although some from the circle would invariably vote for Nixon, the circle stayed strong. And Mom would continue to support the pastor and the church.

That approach to disagreeing but not disappearing from the group has been a lesson well learned from Mom.

After Mandy's death, a woman in our church advised me tearfully that God had told her my vitamin-depleted body was the cause of Mandy's illness. I was so surprised that I said nothing. A few minutes later, I wished that I had told her she needed to let St. Jude's know she had the answer for all of the research into the cause of leukemia. But at the time, I actually thanked her and walked away.

And then a deacon's wife in our church told me in a conversation that was meant to comfort me, "I wonder what you and Earl did to cause Mandy's death." I found no comfort in this question.

The punishment theory was an issue I would have to deal with over time.

I must admit that I had in the most inner parts of my heart wondered about the punishment cause, but I had quickly dismissed it because I did not believe that a God of love would "punish" an innocent child for something I had done.

Hearing another person—someone respected in the church—verbalize the punishment theory caught me off-guard. I didn't answer her then and haven't to this day. Ironically, her life has in the past few years been filled with one tragedy after another. I wonder if she questions herself.

If she asked me that question today, I would tell her that bad things happen because we live in an imperfect world—a "fallen world"— and that life is too short to try to discover a cause for all of its tragedies.

That answer comes from Mom's voice. She taught me to embrace life with zest—the mountains and the valleys. She never doubted that "the God on the mountain, is still God in the valley" (Dartt).

She also taught me to forgive and to let go—to disagree but not to disappear.

These were lessons of forgiveness and hope from and for a Golden Circle, our own—Mom, Mandy, and Me.

Part Three

And Then There Was ... Hope!

Chapter 21

Prayer for the Children

When people ask me how many children I have, I usually respond with, "Two—a daughter and a son—but we raised only one. Our daughter died as an infant of leukemia at St. Jude Children's Research Hospital in Memphis." Some people say they are sorry, and others just change the subject. I never know how to react to either of the responses.

I wonder what kind of person she would have become—born on Thanksgiving Day, 1977. She was beautiful—eight-and-a-half-pounds, jet-black hair, big blue eyes, gentle-white skin. But, the lack of a typical redness in the skin was a mask for the illness. Sometimes what appears to be beautiful can be so ugly when we realize its implications. Maybe prayer is like that—oxymoronic. I prayed to have Mandy, to have a special baby. I often wonder how I would have prayed had I known what I know now—what awaited this tiny being. When I found out I was pregnant again, two years after Mandy's death, I prayed not to have a special baby, just a normal one.

When Mandy was so sick at St. Jude's, she was on many churches' prayer lists, and my students organized a prayer service at one of the local churches just for her. But the prayers for her recovery were not to be answered with a yes. She never even went into remission.

I would sing to her in a room with reverse airflow to keep invading germs out, out of a body that was so wracked by the ravages of cancer that she swelled beyond recognition with the chemo protocol. A protocol influenced by a computer program that would not feel the guilt of failure . . . or the joy of success. There in that room I would sing songs of faith—songs I learned as a child.

Days and nights of prayers for her remission, her cure . . . to no avail. A St. Jude's nurse wrote me after Mandy's death to never place a question mark where God had placed a period. I wonder if she was the same nurse Earl heard saying she just didn't think she could come to work in ICU again: she was so emotionally drained. In December 1977, I remember only five beds in that ICU compound where a doctor was twenty-four hours a day—sleeping there at night. Both Mandy and a young teenager died on Friday, and when we left to come home, a young boy was very critical in the room next to Mandy's. Two out of five —maybe three out of five.

Prayer is a common state to be in when one is the parent of a St. Jude's child. The scriptures say, "Pray without ceasing" (King James Version Bible, 1 Thessalonians 5:17). Many St. Jude's parents know the meaning of that verse—I suspect the parents of all sick children know the meaning. How many times I wanted to just be taken from the pressures and sadness of being a St. Jude's parent during the time of Mandy's stay, especially the ominous knocks on the door in the middle of the night—signifying a potential emergency.

Yes, one learns to pray without ceasing, especially when a daughter's nurse declares, "I can't stick this baby one more time," and my response to the child's screaming terror at the sight of the needle is, "Do it if there's any chance to help her."

I remember standing at the corridor windows and looking out over the interstate in sight of St. Jude's . . . thinking just how could people be going to work, to sports events, to shopping malls, to Christmas parties, to family dinners when my daughter was dying. I wondered what they were praying about . . . praying for.

Prayer did reward me with Mandy; prayer did not stop her dying or the aching of my arms to hold her after her body was buried; prayer did sustain me when all else failed. As Father Brian, the Catholic priest who comforted us, said, "The angels broke through the roof of St. Jude's and carried her to heaven." Yet, as he spoke those words, I did not comprehend what I would later come to accept: The Great Physician lovingly healed Mandy. But at that moment, I wanted to join her! Had I, I would have never known my Isaac (Zac), named after Abraham and Sarah's Isaac! A child who is waited for, loved beyond measure, and dedicated to God by parents.

I can't write too much about Mandy and St. Jude's without being emotionally bankrupted. So, my thoughts often turn to Zac, another prayer child given to us—tested weekly then monthly then yearly for his white blood count.

Just as I can't think of Mandy without tears, I can't think of Zac without smiles. Our Zac—weighing in two weeks early at almost ten pounds, ready to put on a helmet and play football according to some of the onlookers at the baby window where others had marveled at Mandy's beauty.

With Zac, I prayed—with many prayers of thanksgiving and petitions for wisdom in raising him: this bright, confident joy of my life.

I remember when Zac was about three years old and he decided that he was old enough to give his own order over the intercom at one of the local fast-food places. But upon giving his order, the woman on the other end of the intercom replied, "Madam, please order for your child. I cannot understand him."

Now, I understood him perfectly, but I gave his order and watched in the mirror as he pouted in his little car seat. When we got to the window, the woman was feeling bad that she had fussed about his order, so she tried to give him some balloons and toys, but he would not accept anything.

As we pulled out of the drive-in, my son declared, "I hate her."

And I said, "Oh, no, we are <u>not</u> to hate people. We are supposed to love people.

She was just having a bad day; we should forgive her."

We rode home in silence, unpacked the sacks with our lunch and put it on the table. I thought that this was a good time for some teaching about prayer; so I said, "Son, when we have the blessing, why don't you pray for that lady at the fast-food restaurant?"

He said, "Okay," and I just beamed because I knew I had taught him well! He put those sweet little hands together, and said, "Dear God . . . Fire her! Amen."

I said, "Oh, no! That's not how you should pray for her."

He said, "You pray the way you want, and I'll pray the way I want!"

And he ate his sandwich—secure justice would prevail.

I learned very quickly that parents should "pray without ceasing" for healthy children too.

There was little prayer for justice where Mandy was concerned. Her health problems were no result of her doing. The doctors said they believed she was born with leukemia—congenital leukemia—one in a million. Its ugly symptoms were evident by the time she was only a few days old, even though the medical community missed them.

If anyone should be judged by justice, I am that person. I struggled with the questions where did I go, what did I eat, what did I breathe, what did I do that exposed her to an element that triggered the wild multiplication of the white cells in her blood. Not long after Mandy died, there was a news report on hair dye being linked to cancer and the warning not to use such dye during pregnancy. I panicked—spent many nights worrying over whether the hair dye I used during Mandy's pregnancy had been the cause for her congenital leukemia. One day in the depths of despair, I followed Earl's advice and called the health agency whose number had been listed in the news report. The far-away voice on the phone listed the offending dyes—none of which I had ever used. One cause—eliminated from my long list of guilty pleas. Later when eating bacon was accused of causing some types of cancer, Earl convinced me that I had to stop this crusade for finding what caused Mandy's leukemia. Maybe there was no definable reason at this time, and when one would be found someday, I must remember that I had not known that I was introducing this insidious menace to my unborn child.

I suppose all parents who lose children in death must look for reasons—a cause-and-effect expedition that is driven by the perceived need to know. Then, of course, there are those dear people who readily have the answer as to why a child died and are most willing to enlighten bereaved parents. I specifically remember a young college student on campus, like the wife of one of our church deacons, alluding to people were wondering what Earl and I had done that had caused Mandy to be born with leukemia. She was not referring to health issues. And . . . deep in my heart, I knew I had asked the same question. It was easy to judge people for their condemnation but much harder to admit the very same thoughts had entered my mind.

What a treasure the words of Jesus in John 9 when the man born blind was brought to Him and He was asked who had sinned—the parents or the child! With omniscience, He answered that neither had brought on this blindness but that it was an opportunity that God's power could be shown in Him (King James Version Bible, John 9:3). I took great encouragement in the response of Jesus, but always deep in my heart a wisp of wonder never left. And even when two people shared the positive religious impact of Mandy's death on their lives, I went home and tearfully proclaimed to the walls that I would not have given my Mandy for either of them.

Guilt—my guilt—yes, I certainly carried that cup with me for many years. Perhaps in the deepest recesses of my heart, it hides —waiting for a moment to relive itself, but, for now, it does not reveal its sinister existence.

And speaking of justice—what about God? The day Mandy died with thousands of prayers for her life, we were told of a news report that a mother had thrown her newborn out of their hospital window. Was God there? Did He hear a four-year-old's pleas to be rocked by his aging grandmother—separated from him by thick walls of St. Jude glass—connected only by the intercom from the parent-to-patient rooms? Did He see a father crying in the public bathroom after a midnight run to Kentucky Fried Chicken for his daughter's desired delicacy during a lull in nausea—only to return to her chemo-heaving? Did He see me choosing a casket when I should have been choosing toys for Christmas morning? Where was He in this mire of human misery?

My emotions have run the gamut—doom, despondency, anger, and indifference. I often clutched to my very being the words of the pastor at Mandy's funeral: "God is too good to be unkind and too wise to make mistakes." As time has passed, I have made war on that statement, found comfort in it, and accepted that most of what happens here in this fallen world is just far beyond me. Without understanding came a truce of surrender and a step of faith in a loving God—the God of Psalm 56:8. You have "Put my tears into Your bottle . . ." (New King James Version Bible).

JUSTICE TOOK on a whole new meaning with the birth of Zac.

Chapter 22

Prayer for the Child

My mom wanted a grandson from the first time I told my parents that we were pregnant—Dad, a granddaughter.

In 1979, when I was pregnant with Zac, the sonogram was just breaking into rural hospitals in our area. Only because of medical problems was one ordered for us, and a local hospital's pictures were not definitive. So, our obstetrician referred us to Vanderbilt. Prayers abounded for this unborn child. After a team there reviewed the sonogram results, the specialist assured us we had a healthy baby—but a very big baby. When we asked if the sonogram showed the baby's sex, we were told yes. For whatever reason, we did not pursue whether the child was a boy or a girl—we just rejoiced and relaxed in the diagnosis of a healthy baby, an answer to prayer.

So Mom was delighted when she got the call that she had a grandson.

From the first time she held him, there was a bond that they shared until her death when he was 14 years old. From shelling butterbeans in the backyard swing to running from a snake slithering through her flower garden to cooking mac and cheese for a savory treat at the kitchen table, this little boy had a grandmother who adored him! And any problem was often shared over the phone with Gangar—his name for her—before I was told of its existence.

So it is not surprising that one mid-October night when he was five years old and spending the night at his grandparents that his request to put up the Christmas tree at her house was granted. She and Dad went to the attic and got the Christmas tree, the lights, and all of the decorations. After a couple of hours of work, Mom and Zac had decorated that tree and then lit the living room with its bubble lights galore. In fact, to Zac's delight, the double windows across the front of the house revealed the tree's beauty to those who passed by—even though the rest of the street's houses sported Halloween pumpkins, witches, and brooms.

A few days after Zac's visit with his grandparents, one of the clients of Mom's hairstylist broached the subject of Mom's mental health.

"Is Virginia Stoker dealing with early stages of dementia?" she queried Mrs. Jozelle.

"No! Why do you ask such a question?"

"Well..."

"She was in here the other day for her regular appointment and seemed just fine."

"She may be fine to you, but the other night I passed her house, and she had her Christmas tree up and lit."

Mrs. Jozelle laughed. "Oh, I'm sure that's just Zac! She'll do anything he wants!"

And she did—supporting and cheering him on at public speaking competitions, awards ceremonies, and church musicals! Even when she was in the hospital with critical heart problems, she insisted we leave and take him to a regional Optimist speaking competition fifty miles away, which we did and where he won the trophy that graced her Intensive Care cubicle when he returned!

And it was from my mother, the woman who did not achieve her career but sacrificed for me, that Zac gained an early appreciation for and commitment to social justice and equal rights. That appreciation and commitment have been and continue to be at the heart of who he is today.

Yes, I have prayed often about Zac's sense of justice—justice for all. It began to unveil itself when he was in elementary school.

One day Zac came home and announced that a grave injustice was being committed by the teacher in one of his classes. At that time the elementary students were moved from teacher to teacher for about three of their subjects. Zac described how one teacher had both homeroom and subject class rules that were the same. She kept a list of students' names on her bulletin board, and each infraction of rules committed by a student brought a swift mark by his or her name.

Zac presented his argument to me in elevated lawyer vocabulary, an argument that the teacher was invoking double jeopardy. His friend was experiencing the potential, and evidently the assurance, of receiving marks during homeroom activities and then again in the subject class—a condition not faced by most of the students who were coming in from other homerooms. Thus, at the end of the week when candy and small toy rewards were issued, his friend was usually empty-handed.

Zac petitioned me to call or write the teacher about this grave injustice. Listening carefully and determining that Zac was not the victim of the double jeopardy, I suggested he recommend that his friend get his mother to write a letter to the teacher explaining this particular view of the situation and requesting that his misdeeds be placed on two separate charts. Certainly, such mistreatment could not be overlooked, and a caring teacher would quickly rectify the situation and bring justice.

"But, Mom . . . you don't understand . . . he didn't mention this problem to me; he hasn't even realized yet that he is being mistreated. I thought I would tell him tomorrow when we get a plan of action."

Over the years, Zac's sense of justice and commitment to justice for all have been at the heart of many of my prayers.

We always shared with Zac, two years younger than Mandy, that he had a sister. Even though she died before he was born, we knew that others familiar with our family would purposefully or inadvertently mention Mandy to Zac. We did not want him to find out about her life and death from others. I had had a friend in college who had experienced that shock as a ten-year-old and always held the issue against her parents. So, we determined to leave one picture of Mandy out on the mantle and to mention her from time to time when it was appropriate.

When Zac was only two, a television camera crew filmed at our home a segment of a St. Jude Children's Hospital telethon. When the telethon representative arrived, Zac, dressed in a treasured crumpled cowboy hat, cowboy boots, and flannel pajamas, greeted her at the front door. His wide smile and immediate curiosity at the visitors in his home marked him for spontaneous friendship. Mandy's picture opened the segment in which Earl and I expressed the joy and heartache of having a beautiful baby who was later diagnosed with acute leukemia. Zac played among the cameras the crew had brought and, of course, won their hearts —making Mandy's tragedy even more poignant and painful to them.

We knew that once this telethon hit the airways Mandy's tragedy would be both a local and national story. Actually, one Sunday morning we received a call from a long-lost cousin in Michigan who had just seen Mandy's story on the telethon and declared to his own children sitting at the breakfast table and watching TV that those people on screen were their relatives in Tennessee.

And we were right about the need for telling Zac. When he was in elementary school, a mother of one of his classmates told me that when her son questioned her about how it feels to lose someone to death, she told him to ask Zac since his sister died. I was amazed that such a question would be referred to a child, but I guess many parents avoid the discussion of death using whatever means to sidestep the issue.

And, Zac seemed to be more mature and thoughtful than most children. I remember when he was attending the University Nursery School, a pre-kindergarten half-day program that was under the auspices of the University of Tennessee at Martin's College of Education. Zac was always amazing the faculty and us —usually in a positive way. Once when I was taking him home from the morning's classes, he broke the silence in the car with a monstrous sigh.

"What's wrong, Son?"

"Mama, the teachers are teaching us to count ," he complained.

"Well, what's wrong with that? Everybody needs to know how to count."

"It's so boring to count; I want them to talk with me about what number there is beyond which one cannot count."

For the first time, I realized just how special was this child I had prayed to be ordinary.

Zac had seen Mandy's baby picture next to his all of his life. So her existence was just natural to him, a fact that at times caused his teachers' trepidation.

On another day at pre-kindergarten, he created a real stir among the teachers (both faculty and student teachers). It seems that one student teacher had asked the children to describe their brothers and sisters in a talk-time group. I don't know if this particular student teacher had perused the children's records, which would have listed Mandy as a deceased sister, but with questionable thought of the potential consequences for her inquiry, she listened as the children gave responses.

By the time I arrived to pick up Zac at lunch when the morning program ended, the teachers were in quite a flurry.

It seems when four-year-old Zac had responded to the question, he introduced the group to his sister Mandy who lived in heaven with Jesus but was just as surely his sister as any others discussed that day. Ironically, with the teachers wiping tears, the children saw Mandy as the celebrity sibling and treated Zac with the dignity deserved as relative of a star. I often wondered how many went home and declared that they wished they had brothers and sisters like Zac's.

A year later when asked in kindergarten to make a family tree, Zac again brought his teacher to tears by his unquestioned acceptance of his place in a family of unseen children. The teacher called me that night to share that Zac's tree had a limb for Earl, for me, for Mandy, and for himself.

Additionally, there were two unidentified limbs that the teacher, a close friend of mine, had assumed were for Zac's beloved Gangar and Gangi, his grandparents.

When the teacher mentioned Gangar and Gangi, Zac immediately corrected her. Those two limbs were his mommy's babies who died before birth. I suppose those babies were on his mind because one was lost the month that Zac was starting kindergarten—the other two years earlier.

One day a six-year-old Zac asked me why out of all of my children had he lived. I told him I didn't know—it must mean he is truly special. And . . . surely, he is! But what a burden for a child to carry.

To help ease that burden, we had daily morning devotions

throughout Zac's childhood and teenage years. Truly, those times when each of us prayed in that family circle made it possible for that burden to be carried—not lifted, but carried.

Mandy's death was the heaviest hurt for me—a cut to my heart that is so deep no scar can cover it. I have always felt guilty that Zac at such a young age had to be privy to so much hurt. And with that hurt, prayer was a necessity.

A friend of mine shared with me: "It's scriptural; 'joy comes in the morning' (King James Version Bible, Psalms 30:5). It may not be tomorrow morning, but eventually one morning, joy will come." It is that assurance and hope that kept me going many years ago; and, yes, joy did come again in the child Isaac. Perhaps more joy—because of Mandy.

Epilogue

It has been more than forty years since I walked out of the doors of St. Jude Children's Research Hospital on a December night approaching Christmas, and at times it seems as if it were only yesterday.

Often when we travel through Memphis, Interstate 40 carries us by St. Jude's on Danny Thomas Boulevard. I look up at the windows where I once stood looking down at the cars on Interstate 40. I see how the hospital has expanded to include other tall buildings and huge parking areas. The sick children keep coming—some for cure, some for remission, and some to "burst through the roof in the arms of angels."

But all come for the hope the nurse told me of that night so long ago.

IN THE YEARS since Mandy's death, I have come to a greater appreciation and understanding of the words the nurse greeted me with that late night in December of 1977. The only hope I considered at the time was the hope for Mandy to be cured. But I found more hope there than just that primary hope for healing.

I found the hope that comes from desiring just one more day of being together with someone I love. Someone had asked me when Mandy was born what I was going to do about my commitment to my profession. My mom had left her profession for me, and I had seen the emptiness from that decision that haunted her. So, what would I do? I flippantly answered that someone else could take care of Mandy as well as I could, and we would just work together. No other child that I would conceive would ever be looked at in that light again. Although I worked in my profession throughout the majority of my son's life, I cherished every moment I was with him. And as we watched him learn and grow, I knew no one would care for him the way we would.

I found the hope for treasured moments—moments that would bind me with those I love. Precious moments with my husband, my son, my grandchildren. Precious memories of Mom, Dad, Mandy. I never leave family members now without telling them I love them. I am very aware of no promise of tomorrow.

I found the hope to be happy again. At first, I felt guilty for wanting to be happy again, but I now know that our psyche can only take so much sorrow. We cannot survive overwhelming sadness forever. I eventually allowed myself to feel moments of happiness. And, at some point—I don't know when—the happy moments began to outnumber the sad ones.

I found hope for other children like my Mandy—children with catastrophic illnesses. Some of the greatest honors we have paid Mandy's life were when our family did a national telethon and when we participated in local and regional radio-thons for St. Jude's. Many have given financially in honor of her over the last forty years.

And that hope for children with leukemia in today's world is manifested in recent St. Jude Children's Research Hospital statistics for children with ALL (acute lymphoblastic leukemia). "St. Jude has led the way in how the world treats childhood leukemia since the hospital opened in 1962. St Jude patients with ALL have a 94% survival rate" ("Acute Lymphoblastic Leukemia").

I found hope for parents who don't realize what a joy they have in their children. I often advise parents to go home and hug their children. I hope for a reality check for those apathetic or uncaring parents, and I take every opportunity to express that hope to them, even to the extent that Earl has had to pull me to another aisle at the local Wal-Mart when parents are tongue-lashing or ignoring their children.

I found hope I can offer to those who are grieving for a child or parent who has died. As a teacher at a university, I have often come across students who have suffered the loss of a parent. My heart is for both a parent who has a child who has died and a child whose parent has died. Because of Jesus, there is hope to offer. In my spiritual journey, I have come to the place where I grieve, but not as "others who have no hope" (New King James Version Bible, 1 Thessalonians 4:13).

I found hope in a medical profession that at first had failed us with poor diagnosis and even disdain at our insistence that something was wrong with our baby. At St. Jude's we found the best representatives of medicine, both professionally and personally. The letters and cards from the ICU nurses after Mandy died were compassionate and encouraging. And her doctor's hand-written letter, which follows, is a treasure that even today offers us comfort on days and nights of grief.

2 January 78
Dear Earl and Jenna Wright,

I cannot tell you how sorry I am about Mandy. I was informed about her catastrophic event too late to be of any comfort to you. As is unfortunately the case, little children can do very badly, very suddenly. All of the known problems were under control. What happened to her was unavoidable—it could not be anticipated, and nothing could have been done to prevent it or correct it. Massive pulmonary hemorrhages are catastrophic; usually sudden, without warning, and almost always fatal. Mandy was a strong fighter and other problems were under control, but this was too much for her and us. We know to expect anything during the first two weeks, especially with very young children, but we had not seen this problem in many years. The cause was undoubtedly her leukemia—although the counts were coming under control, she still had a massive amount of disease left.

I am sure she felt no pain with this, since children usually go into shock when it occurs. All the blood and platelets in the world could not prevent or help with this problem.

Although she had a significant chance of coming through the years of treatment, it would have been a long up-hill battle all the way, and numerous complications could have taken her from us along the way. At any rate, I am sorry that more could not be done, but as *you told me you were prepared for the worst, and we know she is happy with God now.*

I hope you two were able to enjoy the holidays with your family, and will at some time again think about more family of your own. She was a beautiful product of two lovely people—the world could use more of you.

God bless you both.
Gary Brodeur, MD

AND, yes, I did allow myself the hope of another child. When we went back to St. Jude's to talk with the doctors in March after Mandy's death, we were told that although her leukemia was thought to be congenital, it would be highly unlikely that we would have another child with congenital cancer. Two years and two days after her birth, her brother Isaac (Zac) was born. Although he was tested every month for the first year of his life, he never showed any signs of leukemia. He is the joy of our lives today. We were pregnant twice after Zac's birth—both pregnancies ending in the death of the babies before birth.

I also allowed myself to find the hope of many "adopted" children when we became the directors of the University Department of First Baptist Church, Martin, in February 1978, only two months after Mandy's death. God had in store for us hundreds, yes even thousands, of university students who over the next forty years would become "our children" through the University ministry. And Isaac would be blessed with the joy of brothers and sisters from around the world. We "adopted" many of the international and American students formally through the church's Adopt-a-Student Program and many informally as they found their way into our home and our hearts. Even my mom and dad were delighted to be the "adopted" grandparents of one international son who honored us as his parents at his wedding in the States.

I found hope in love—not just hope in others' love for me, which has often sustained me in this journey, but hope that I can see with the eyes of Jesus and love others. As 1 John 4:7, 8 declares, "Beloved, Let us love one another; for love is of God; and everyone that loveth is born of God, and knoweth God. He that loveth not knoweth not God; for God is love" (King James Version Bible).

Finally, I found hope for seeing Mom, Dad, and Mandy in a joyous reunion one day. Jesus said, "I am the resurrection and the life. He who believes in Me, though he may die, he shall live" (New King James Version Bible, John 11:25). So, when the angels carry me home, I hope to see a little baby standing there with tiny open hands waiting to clutch my fingers.

I HAVE COME to realize in the years since Mandy died that all that life really has to offer is hope. And, so I say, "Read . . . this really is a story of hope."

The beginning verses of Joshua 4 call us to set stones of remembrance—memorials to times when God has shown himself intimately to us, memorials to strengthen our faith by reminding us that God is always with us, yes in both triumph and tragedy. The writer of Joshua says, "when your children ask in time to come, saying, 'What do these stones mean to you?' . . . And these stones shall be for a memorial . . ." (New King James Version Bible, Joshua 4:6,7). They are a reminder.

My prayer is that this book is a stone of remembrance—a reminder of hope—for all who read it.

Sources Cited

"Acute Lymphoblastic Leukemia (ALL)." 2024. <u>St. Jude Children's Research Hospital</u>. July 2024 <https://www. stjude.org/disease/acute-lymphoblastic-leukemia-all.html>.

Brodeur, Gary. Letter to Earl and Jenna Wright. 2 January 1978.

Dartt, Tracy G. Lyrics to "God on the Mountain." <u>SongLyrics</u>. https://www.songlyrics.com/bill-gloria-gaither/god-on-the-mountain-lyrics/.

King James Version Bible. Norwalk, Connecticut: The C.R. Gibson Company, 1958.

Miller, Thomas, and Mark Harris. Lyrics to "Grace That Won't Let Go." <u>Word to Worship</u>. https://wordstoworship.com/song/14548.

New International Version Bible. Grand Rapids, Michigan: Zondervan, 1978.

New King James Version Bible. Nashville: Thomas Nelson Publishers, 1982.

Tindley, Charles A. "When the Morning Comes." <u>Baptist Hymnal 1975</u>, Convention Press, 1975, p. 499.

Wright, Jenna Stoker. "Escape in a Rocking Chair." <u>Flashlight Memories</u>. Ed. Ginny Greene, <u>et al</u>. Abilene, Texas: Silver Boomer Books, 2011. 211-212.

About the Author

Jenna Stoker Wright, who grew up in Gleason, Tennessee, is a retired associate professor of English and chair of the Department of English and Modern Foreign Languages at UT Martin. She has her BA, MS, and MFA with an extensive list of scholarly and creative activities. At UT Martin, she was a Smith Professorship Endowment recipient and has received numerous teaching awards and honors, including the UT Martin Coffey Outstanding Teacher Award, the UT National Alumni Association Outstanding Teacher Award, the UT Martin Outstanding Educator Award, and the National Society of Leadership and Success Excellence in Teaching Award. At UT Martin, Jenna served as president of the Faculty Senate and on the UT System Faculty Council.

Jenna Wright and her husband, Earl, served as co-directors of the University Sunday School Department (a Bible study life group for college students) at the First Baptist Church of Martin, Tennessee, for over forty years (from February 1978 until July 2018).

Included here is her personal faith testimony, "From Tragedy to Treasure," which she has presented at college student retreats, BCM worship groups, and churches throughout the area.

She is married to Earl Wright and has one son, Isaac "Zac" Wright, and two granddaughters, Grace Wright and Isobel Wright.

She makes her home in Martin, Tennessee.

From Tragedy to Treasure
The Testimony of Jenna Stoker Wright

"For I am not ashamed of the gospel of Christ: for it is the power of God unto salvation to every one that believeth . . . " (King James Version Bible, Romans 1:16).

I grew up in a Christian home where both mother and father attended church. As a small child, I became a church member, but I became concerned about my relationship with Jesus as I grew older and dealt with this concern for several years. Throughout all of this time, I continued to the best of my ability to try to be like my concept of Jesus. I thank God for watching over me through those years.

I was an organized person who wanted to control life and whatever situations I found myself in at the moment. I found more and more things in life I could not control. And in 1977, those uncontrollable situations came to an apex. Our first child, Mandy, was born with congenital leukemia and died at St. Jude Children's Hospital after three weeks of life. After her death, I would share with friends that I was learning wonderful concepts about Jesus. And I was—but there is a difference in knowing concepts about Jesus's love and knowing Him as Lord and Savior.

In 1983, following a revival series at our church, six years after Mandy's death, I could not shake this desire to have peace about me and my life. I wanted to know Jesus personally—I wanted someone who could take control of my life.

I looked at the materials shared at the revival service and read

Romans 3:23. "For all have sinned, and come short of the glory of God" (King James Version Bible). I am a sinner. We all are. Sin is an "I" controlled life.

I read Romans 6:23. "For the wages of this sin is death; but the gift of God is eternal life through Jesus Christ our Lord" (King James Version Bible). Sin's penalty is being separated from God in this life and the life to come, but God gives the gift of eternal life through Jesus. When He went to the cross, He took our sin, accepted the judgment for it, and made it possible for us to be accepted by God.

I read Acts 3:19. "Repent ye therefore, and be converted, that your sins may be blotted out. . . " (King James Version Bible). Repentance is turning from sin and turning to God through Jesus. Ephesians 2:8 says, "For by grace are ye saved through faith; and that not of yourselves: it is the gift of God" (King James Version Bible). Faith is trusting in Jesus! Nothing more, nothing less, and nothing else!

I read Romans 10: 9, 10. "If you declare with your mouth, 'Jesus is Lord,' and believe in your heart that God raised him from the dead, you will be saved. For it is with your heart that you believe and are justified, and it is with your mouth that you profess your faith and are saved" (New International Version Bible).

All night I thought on those scriptures that I had read. The next afternoon in prayer, I asked for Jesus to come into my life with what little faith I could muster. I asked Him to forgive me. I accepted Him as everything He is—Savior and Lord!

And I have the assurance of John 1:12. "Yet to all who did receive him, to those who believed in his name, he gave the right to become children of God" (New International Version Bible).

So you see, I went from tragedy to treasure. As tragic as the death of our daughter is, that is not the tragedy to which I refer. I speak of the tragedy of not knowing Jesus to the treasure of knowing Him as Lord and Savior!

And now . . . "I know whom I have believed and am persuaded that *he* [emphasis added] is able to keep that which I have committed unto him against that day" (King James Version Bible, 2 Timothy 1:12).

www.ingramcontent.com/pod-product-compliance
Lightning Source LLC
Chambersburg PA
CBHW020005050426
42450CB00005B/320